Psycholinguistics in the Schools

Phyllis L. Newcomer

Donald D. Hammill

Charles E. Merrill Publishing Company
A Bell & Howell Company
Columbus, Ohio

Published by
Charles E. Merrill Publishing Company
A Bell & Howell Company
Columbus, Ohio 43216

This book was set in Palatino and Optima.
The Production Editor was Lynn Walcoff.
The cover was designed by Will Chenoweth.

Library of Congress Catalog Card Number: 75-13354

International Standard Book Number: 0-675-08677-9

2 3 4 5—80 79 78 77 76

Printed in the United States of America

9/27/76 phl. F. 36

Contents

Figures

Tables

Preface

The purpose of this book is to survey the impact of psycholinguistic concepts on educational practice. In so doing, we have presented a brief overview of several psycholinguistic theories, including the ideas of B. F. Skinner, Charles Osgood, and Noam Chomsky. However, since our book is designed for educators seeking information about psycholinguistic theory that has been applied most directly to school instructional activities, we have chosen to focus our discussion on Osgood's theoretical contributions. Osgood's concepts underlie the curricula of many teacher training programs in special education, provide a basis for numerous instructional packages (e.g. the Peabody Language Development Kit), and constitute the foundations of the Illinois Test of Psycholinguistic Abilities, perhaps the most popular psychoeducational diagnostic device used in the schools today.

In practice, the educator's approach to psycholinguistics is based upon three assumptions: (1) that psycholinguistic constructs are measurable by *available tests* and therefore their evaluation can lead to differential diagnosis of an individual's psycholinguistic strengths and weaknesses; (2) that psycholinguistic constructs, as measured, are related directly to school failure, i.e., such deficits cause or contribute to academic difficulties, rather than merely predict them; and (3) that once identified, the specific psycholinguistic problems are remediable by programs or techniques which are *readily available*. Each chapter in this book deals with one of these assumptions.

We have attempted to avoid unnecessary theoretical discourses and deductive arguments. Instead, we have focused primarily on presentations of the research that relates to these topics; we have chosen to deal with the actual data-base underlying each of the three assumptions. Our particular analysis of the data resulted in our reaching what is essentially a nonadvocacy position regarding the practical educational usefulness of the principle test, the ITPA, and training programs which represent the Osgood model. Although we believe that our conclusions are based on a reasonably objective interpretation, we recognize the fact that many professionals would not agree with us. Therefore, to be fair, we decided to expose our readers to alternate points of view. We invited three individuals who have been identified as strong advocates of the Osgood related approach to psycholinguistics in education, Drs. Esther Minskoff, Wilma Jo Bush, and John McLeod, to respond to our work and to present their particular positions. We would like to thank our friendly "adversaries" for their valuable contributions to our book.

P. Newcomer
D. Hammill

Application of Psycholinguistics to Education

Introduction

Individuals who would assess language abilities in children and plan specific instructional programs in their behalf should have at least a superficial grasp of psycholinguistics. While extensive reading of primary sources is desirable, we have attempted to present in this chapter a brief overview of the major underlying premises of the field. These consist primarily of important contributions from linguistics and psychology and include the major theoretical positions influencing education today.

Basic Principles Comprising Psycholinguistics

Psycholinguistics is the study of the mental processes which underlie the acquisition and use of language. As such, it is clearly the progeny of a rather unruly marriage between psychology, the study of behavior, and linguistics, the study of language structure. As is the case in most marriages between two strong partners, there are frequent disputes over who has contributed most to the offspring and over whose position is dominant. A brief synopsis of both points of view should demonstrate to the reader the nature of each discipline's approach to language and the components of each which were absorbed in the evolution of the new discipline, psycholinguistics.

The Linguistic Contribution

The conceptualization of a grammar that encompasses the rules by which speech sounds and meanings are formulated into sentences is the basic premise of most modern linguists. The development of a linguistic grammar involves the isolation of language universals, i.e., the determination of rules which are applicable to all languages and which can account for the infinite variety of sentences created by man. These rules are actually theoretical explanations which are sufficient to account for the total language knowledge that every individual must possess in order to understand others and to express himself. The reader has probably noted with relief that the linguistic usage of the term *grammar*, which encompasses the rules underlying all utterances, differs from the traditional "public school" use of the term, which relates to forms of expression which constitute "good usage." Deese (1971) has compiled four general rules pertaining to linguistic grammar which should clearly demonstrate its characteristics:

1. A *grammar must generate only sentences*. A grammar cannot include rules that permit the formulation of word sequences such as "Give the to flower friend the."
2. *A grammar must generate an infinite number of sentences*. The rules must account for the fact that man is capable of formulating an endless number of novel sentences.
3. *A grammar must generate an infinite possibility of sentences by applying a finite set of rules to a finite set of symbols*. The rules of the grammar must involve a fixed number of operations on the symbols of the language. For example, in English there are twenty-six letters in the alphabet (a finite number of symbols) which can be manipulated in a definite, rule-governed manner to form words.
4. *A grammar must not impose an arbitrary limit on the length of the sentences*. The rules must simply allow for the repetition of linguistic symbols to form sentences of indefinite length.

In order to investigate grammar more expeditiously, linguists have attempted to isolate its components. We can best examine these grammatic constituents by analyzing their relationships to the strings of linguistic elements referred to as sentences.

A sentence may be said to consist of a series of meaningful units called *morphemes*. In some cases words are morphemes in that they represent basic units of meaning within the sentence. For example, in the sentence "I played ball," the words "I" and "ball" are morphological forms. The word "played," however, represents two morphemes, i.e., "play" and the suffix "ed." The use of the suffix alters meaning to the extent that it places the action of play in the past. Consequently the suffix is a distinct element which influences meaning and can be considered a morpheme. Obviously it is not necessary for a morpheme to stand independently within a sentence. Any inflection, i.e., prefix, suffix, etc., which can be attached to a word form and change its meaning is a morpheme.

The reader may have noted by now that it is possible to string together a collection of morphemes without forming acceptable sentences, i.e., sentences which convey the user's meaning to others. For example, "The people of happy work enjoyed their group" contains a string of morphemes, but it is anomalous, or senseless. Obviously another component of grammar is needed to account for the manner in which sentences are ordered. The term *syntax* is used to explain the rules which govern sentence formation, i.e., the positions and relationships of the morphemes involved in the sentence. For example, if the string of words presented above is ordered to read "The group of happy people enjoyed their work," it can be assumed that the speaker's underlying awareness of syntactic rules provided the structure for the correct organization of all morphemes. Although syntactic rules are apparently mastered at a relatively early age, people are not aware of their existence, i.e., they cannot state them.

Another component of language which has been extensively studied by linguists is *phonology*, the science of significant speech sounds. *Phoneme* is the term used to describe the sounds produced by the vocalization of letters or combinations of letters which alter the meanings of the words in which they are used. For example, if the sound connected with the letter "r" is substituted for "b" in the word "best," the word becomes "rest" and the meaning is changed. Consequently both /r/ and /b/ are phonemes or significant speech sounds.

Linguists have performed comprehensive analyses of sound and have been able to categorize all significant English sounds into approximately thirty-six phonemes. The major distinguishing feature among them is between those designated as vowels and those called consonants, a distinction which depends in part upon the position of the tongue and the extent to which the flow of air through the mouth cavity is unimpeded. Vowels and consonants have been classified further, such as front and back vowels or as stop and fricative consonants, and rules for their usage have been developed.

The final element of importance to linguists is *semantics*, the study of meaning. This investigation involves not only the manner in which meaning becomes associated with morphological or phonological forms, but also the rules which determine the manner in which meaning is conveyed within the sentence. It is easily demonstrated that it is possible to formulate morphologically and syntactically accurate sentences which are semantically incomplete in that they do not clearly convey meaning. For example, "They were throwing up" is an ambiguous sentence. The message could refer to the behavior of the subject in hurling an object in a particular direction or to an act of regurgitation. In many cases the semantic interpretation of a sentence depends upon the context in which it occurs.

Generally speaking, linguists have concentrated on structured approaches to semantics and have attempted to analyze the denotative meanings of words in order to find their common dimension. The theory which underlies this approach is that words which share many common dimensions approximate each other in meaning and may be used in similar fashion. For example, the words *man, male, boy,* and *lad* share the component of "sex," and there is a degree of similarity in their meaning and use. The words *boy* and *lad* share the component of age as well as sex. Following the logic of the theory that shared components increase similarity in meaning, the words *boy* and *lad* are closer in meaning and can be more freely substituted for each other.

The most apparent weakness in this method of analysis is that its applicability is limited. It is most efficient when used to categorize concrete referent classes which are discretely different. For example, the component "sex" is an easily determined distinction for words such as "boy" and "girl." Many words, however, are not marked by such obviously distinct characteristics. It is difficult to categorize such relatively ambiguous terms as "liberty," "equality," etc.

Although the topic of semantics has been investigated for many years, theorists have reached no agreement as to how word meanings develop. There are even fewer conclusions about the manner in which word meanings are formed into sentence meanings. In fact, if any single component is responsible for the interrelation of psychological and linguistic theory for the study of psycholinguistics, it is the importance of investigating the psychological processes involved in the development of meaning. Further exploration of this subject brings our discussion to the psychological contribution to psycholinguistics.

The Psychological Contribution

Among psychologists, knowledge of the mental processes which make learning possible is perceived as a preeminent consideration in understanding language. In other words, the psychological frame of reference involves the manner in which children acquire, store, retrieve, and use information. To account for the mentalistic abilities involved in processing language information, many psychologists have devised complex theoretical models which explore the sensory and perceptual behaviors involved in the reception of stimuli, the activities of the nervous system in the storage memory of information and its retrieval, and the manner in which these systems interact to build meaningful associations. Psychologists also have considered the importance of variables which are indirectly related to language, such as attention and motivation of the learner, as well as external components, such as stimulus value. In psychological theory all variables which affect linguistic competence are important to understanding language development. From this point of view, the rules of a language have significance only insofar as they apply to the manner in which an individual uses the language. Psychologists are concerned with the intrinsic components of human behavior which govern the development and utilization of language patterns.

It is quite logical therefore that their research is focused mostly on the study of semantics. Historically, the psychological approach to semantics has involved investigations of the mentalistic processes responsible for the linkage of meaning with various symbols. In other words, psychologists have generated hypotheses about those activities in the brain which cause learning. Explanations of this phenomenon have varied from Titchner's *Structuralism,* which involved the conceptualization of "mental images" observable through introspection, to Watson's *Behaviorism,* which focused on observable peripheral responses as reflections of internal behaviors, e.g., barely perceptible movements of speech mechanisms representing thought. The majority of psychological theory is primarily neobehavioristic in that while it expands the stimulus–response paradigm, which was originally designed to explain observable external responses, it also invites conjectures of implicit S–R connections which account for activities in the brain. Generally, theories which explain behavior in terms of the relationships between stimuli and responses (S–R) may be included under the rubric of *Associationism.* It is from this psychological context that the most popular semantic theory has emerged. Although there are many variations, most of these associationistic conceptualizations may be classified into two types— theories of reference and theories of use.

Referential theory suggests that the meaning of a word is that object to which it refers. For example, the word "ball" means "a round object." The most obvious weakness in this theory is that the word "ball" has many additional meanings, e.g., it can denote a good time, as in "I had a ball" or it may denote a particular type of dance as in "I went to the ball." In other words, the same word has varied referents. In addition, a referent could conceivably relate to many words. A young man named "Bill" is also a "boy," a "student," and a "driver." Although the referent is a particular individual and all four words refer to that individual, the words "Bill," "boy," "student," and "driver" do not have the same meaning.

Theories of usage simply imply that meaning is the response a words evokes in the listener. For example, if an individual responds "throw it" to the word "ball," the meaning of "ball" is "that which is thrown." The difficulty with this explanation is that there appears to be a myriad of responses which could be made to the ball, e.g., "it's round," "it's red," "it's mine," "I like it." It would be inappropriate to consider all of these responses as accurate meanings of the word ball.

As the reader can see, neither of these theories is particularly encompassing. In fact, there has been much dispute among psycholinguists over the applicability of the Associationist approaches to language. These objections will be discussed later in greater detail. Suffice it to say that while these positions have obvious limitations, they represent honest attempts to understand the incredibly complex question of meaning development. If nothing more, they provide stimulation for further investigation and make clear the necessity to utilize available information from related fields of study.

Major Psycholinguistic Theories

As the reader may have noted by now, psycholinguistics has not long existed as an independent discipline. Despite its relative novelty, it incorporates input from two schools of thought which have for some time sought to determine how language is developed. Psychological and linguistic research on the topic exists in vast quantities and serves as a base for modern psycholinguistic research. Seemingly, combining common interests from two independent disciplines into psycholinguistics has been beneficial. First, it has emphasized the connection between the rules and form of language usage (the linguistic approach) and the psychological behaviors that influence their development. Second, the emergence of a new field which focuses attention specifically on language as it is used offers a convenient body of knowledge for those professionals who seek to teach language.

It was as recent as 1954 when C. E. Osgood, a psychologist, focused attention on the manner in which children learn language. He and Sebeok edited a book, *Psycholinguistics: A Survey of Theory and Research Problems,* which for all practical purposes gave birth to psycholinguistics as an independent discipline. The ideas conveyed in this volume were innovative in that they dealt with the pertinent area of language acquisition, but for the most part they were formulated with little input from the field of linguistics. Osgood's conceptualizations, in particular, reflected the principles of stimulus–response psychology. This work and similar presentations of S–R theory that followed evoked responses from certain linguists, most notably Noam Chomsky, and indirectly resulted in the merger of these diverse schools of thought into the most modern conception of psycholinguistics. Psychologists who were interested in language simply adopted the ideas presented by Chomsky and his followers and proceeded with their own research. For example, Slobin, a psycholinguist, has applied Chomsky's ideas in his investigations of the language development of Russian children. Indisputably, psycholinguistics, as it exists today, is composed primarily of linguistic theory. The impact of psychology remains specifically focused on the underlying behaviors which relate primarily to the development of semantics. On the whole, one may consider psycholinguistics as *a science which provides for the use of linguistic analysis of grammar to identify the mental and behavioral processes which underlie language acquisition and development.*

Although psycholinguistics is so broadly defined that it includes varied theoretical positions, most of the work, as has been suggested previously, emanates from two major schools of thought. These are Transformational Grammar postulated by Chomsky, a linguist, and an extension of S–R learning theory to language most clearly represented in the work of Skinner and Osgood, behavioral psychologists. As the psychological theory was presented initially and evoked response from Chomsky, we shall examine their respective theoretical positions in the same order.

B. F. Skinner's S–R Theory

In applying the principles of learning theory to language, Skinner and Osgood, among others, have assumed that language learning occurs in the same manner as other types of learning, i.e., from the formation of stimulus–response associations. Words are used in sentences because they are conditioned responses. A thorough examination of Skinner's theories followed by Osgood's extentions of Skinner's model should help clarify the logic behind this point of view.

In his book *Verbal Behavior* (1957), Skinner describes language as operant behavior in that it is emitted without observable stimuli and is controlled by its consequences (reinforcement). He maintains that if the consequence is rewarding, the linguistic behavior increases in frequency. If the behavior is punished in some manner, its occurrence decreases and eventually is extinguished. Consequently children initially learn to emit and respond to the sounds which constitute language because these sounds are associated with positive reinforcement. For example, if a child makes sounds such as "dada" and receives much adult attention (positive reinforcement), he is likely to emit the sound again. As his experiences increase, his behavior is shaped through reinforcement to make the sound in a manner which more closely resembles the adult pronunciation (dada becomes daddy) and to associate that sound with a particular individual. These changes in the child's verbal behavior occur because the adult becomes more selective about the particular behavior he reinforces. Initially the child is reinforced for merely uttering "dada." Later he may be acknowledged only when he associates the word with a male. Finally, he may elicit positive reinforcement only by using the term in reference to a particular male, presumably his father.

Skinner attempts to account for all language development through a list of behaviors which he calls verbal operants. The *mand* is his term to denote the verbal behavior which reduces a drive state, as in a thirsty child learning the word "water." The *tact* is a verbal response to a physical stimulus, as in associating "chair" with the object. *Echoic* behavior refers to duplication of previously heard speech, such as imitating a parent's verbalizations. *Textual* behavior is a verbal response to a graphic symbol, as in pronouncing a written word. Finally, *intraverbal* behavior denotes a response to other verbal behavior or the habitual association of a word with another word, e.g., "bread and butter." Skinner's conceptualizations regarding language acquisition reflect his general theory of learning and deal only with observable behaviors, i.e., overt stimuli and overt responses. He acknowledges no necessity to explain symbolic covert processes (operations in the brain) which occur between observable S and observable R. In other words, he deals with what he can see and measure.

In order to relate this to language, let us examine a typical *mand*. Skinner is content to explain the overt relationship between the utterance of "water" and the drive-reducing reinforcer, a glass of water. He does not attempt to explain in what manner the drive state caused or related to the verbalization or what internal processes are responsible for the child's storage or retrieval of that association for future usage. In fact, he does not posit intervening variables between the overt stimulus and response; consequently he does not attempt to explain the development of meaning, nor does he separate language into expressive and receptive processes.

Insofar as psycholinguistics is concerned, Skinner's ideas about language represent a relatively early attempt to depict language as part of a more encompassing human behavior: learning. Previously language had been most often studied in isolation, e.g., the number of nouns a child uttered per sentence, or as an index of pathology in the study of aphasia. Language represented as simply another learning phenomenon explicable through the "Laws of Conditioning" becomes manageable. In other words, parents and teachers interested in shaping particular language behaviors may do so by following the principles of operant conditioning (reinforcing desirable behaviors). Consequently Skinner's ideas have considerable appeal to educators who believe that their intervention can be a critical determinant of what a child learns or does not learn. The control of contingencies, i.e., "to reinforce or not to reinforce," has indeed become one of the most popular questions asked in schools.

The use of reinforcement techniques to change behavior obviously does not signify that a similar degree of acceptance has been afforded to Skinner's explanation of language development. The fact that a teacher may reward Johnny for correctly using the word "water" in a sentence does not mean she accepts the theory that "water" is a *mand*, i.e., learned in order to reduce thirst, the drive state. In fact, although Skinner's methodology for modifying behavior has great popularity, the educational application of his language theory has been less than overwhelming. The only direct application of the

Skinner model is as the basis for the *Parson Language Sample* (Spradlin, 1963), a diagnostic test which measures vocal (imitating sentences, completing sentences, naming objects) and nonvocal behavior (imitating gestures and following directions). As might be expected of an instrument based on the principles of operant conditioning, the PLS is designed to measure language performance. It does not lend itself to the formulation of elaborate hypotheses about the underlying causes of language deficits. Speech and language are equated as observable responses elicited by positive reinforcement. Perhaps for that reason the PLS is used infrequently in educational research and has not provided the impetus for related programs of language remediation. It seems fair to say that Skinner's linguistic conceptualizations have been much less influential in education than other aspects of his psychological theories.

It is also relevant to reiterate the importance of Skinner's hypotheses as ground-breaking activity since he was one of the first modern psychologists to offer an encompassing theory of language development. The following discussion of the Osgood and Chomsky positions which were initially offered to refute Skinner not only illustrates their points of disagreement with Skinner and each other, but includes most of the constructs which have become incorporated in psycholinguistics.

C. E. Osgood's S–r–s–R Theory

Osgood was critical of Skinner's theories of language acquisition because he felt they were incomplete. Unlike Skinner, he did not consider it appropriate to deal only with external stimuli and responses (those which could be seen and measured). His primary objection to this type of paradigm was its inability to account for meaning, i.e., semantics. He proposed a multistaged model of language behavior which included representations of implicit stimulus and responses mediating between the observable S and R, written S–r–s–R. In other words, he attempted to trace the process which connected the overt S and R by conceptualizing mentalistic activity, i.e., partial responses "r" and stimuli "s" occurring in the brain. Osgood explained the associational process by suggesting that when a primary stimulus is closely followed by the occurrence of a secondary stimulus, the latter evokes a fractional part of the response behavior originally elicited by the primary stimulus.

Let us assume, for example, that a large animal (primary stimulus) has been presented to a child in close association with pronunciation of the word "dog" (secondary stimulus) and that the child has responded to the animal by fleeing. On another occasion when the child encounters the word "dog," it has now become representative of the animal (primary stimulus) and will evoke a fraction of the original response, i.e., a desire to flee. Osgood diagrams this fractional response which occurs within the child as "r," as it is not the overt response "R" which the child actually makes. The next chain in the association occurs when the fractional "r," a mediating process, produces covert self-stimulation which is implicit "s." That is, the partial response evokes new stimulation inside the child. For example, the desire to flee might cause awareness of the absence of a parent. This internal or implicit "s" is also a mediating process because it in turn evokes the observable response (R), crying. A schematic presentation of Osgood's Model of Communication is shown in figure 1.

Relating the S–r–s–R paradigm with Osgood's explanation of meaning, it is the implicit r–s which constitutes the representational process and denotes what the stimulus means. The associations that a

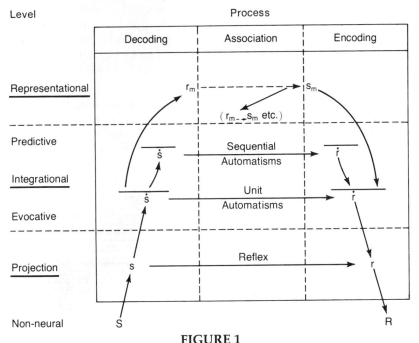

FIGURE 1

Osgood's Model of Communication

stimulus causes in the brain constitute its meaning and evoke cognitive operations, such as abstract reasoning and problem solving. Osgood refers to the symbolic or meaningful aspects of learning as the *representational level* of mental organization.

Although Osgood's conceptualization of the representational (symbolic) level of language is his key postulate, it constitutes but one of three levels of mental organization which complete his linguistic theory. He also proposes an *integrative level* which deals with the processing of nonmeaningful information. The integrative level involves a lower form of language behavior—the associations with stimuli which do not require thought. Examples of this type of language integration might be the short-term sequential memory task of repeating digits or a response involving closure, e.g., an overlearned response such as the last word of a familiar poem. Osgood's third level of organization, the *projection level,* accounts for physiological or reflex behaviors which are of little importance in language acquisition. Osgood's constructs may be more clearly understood by examining figure 1.

Analysis of Osgood's explanation of semantics reveals that it is a form of referential theory. Essentially, all meaning is directly or indirectly associated with a referent, such as the dog in our example. The mediation hypothesis provides for the association of one word with another and eliminates the necessity for direct association with the referent. For example, the word "dog," which originally referred to the actual dog (referent), may now act as a mediating response to new stimulus words, such as "animal" in "The dog is an animal." The word "animal" evokes a fraction of the response in the child which was associated originally with the word "dog," and he may even call all animals "dogs" for a period of time. In this manner, chains of language are formed and may be extended indefinitely.

Osgood's depiction of intervening variables permits him to delineate the processes involved in language behavior as decoding or reception (the S–r relationship), association (the r–s relationship), and encoding or expression (the s–R relationship). To Osgood's way of thinking, the inability to make this type of differentiation using the Skinnerian model (in which there are no intervening variables to separate) constituted a critical inadequacy. He perceived these processes to be distinct and hypothesized that language disability might relate to specific process deficiency. In other words, a child might have normal capacity to receive and associate linguistic stimuli but be deficient in expressive ability (the s–R relationship).

Osgood formulated and attempted to validate many of his

principles through research in aphasia, a disorder of linguistic symbolization. His theories became closely associated with clinical manifestations of language disabilities. He could, for example, specifically delineate the breakdown of mental processes which caused an individual whose speech mechanisms were intact to be unable to name a common object despite his obvious knowledge of the object. In Osgoodian terminology the individual would appear to have a malfunction of expressive ability at the representational (meaningful) level of organization.

It was perhaps due in part to the clinical applicability of Osgood's theories for diagnostic purposes that his ideas attracted considerable attention among educators and educational psychologists. Certainly professionals involved in education had a very practical need to understand the nature of the particular deficit which causes some children to have difficulty acquiring language. In any event, Osgood's conception of psycholinguistics was incorporated in the Illinois Test of Psycholinguistic Abilities (Kirk, McCarthy, and Kirk, 1968), one of the most popular psychometric instruments currently being used in the schools. Consequently, Osgood's theories and Kirk's modification of them have had great influence in education and will be discussed in great detail in a later chapter.

Noam Chomsky's Transformational Grammar

Although the ideas put forth by Skinner and Osgood vary in many particulars, they both reflect the Associationist's belief that the position of each word in a sentence is determined by the word which immediately precedes it. Since each word is a stimulus for the next word, a sentence may be defined as a left-to-right chain of stimulus–response associations. For example, in the sentence *"The boy ran,"* *the* is positioned first because it is usually used to begin a sentence; *the* acts as a stimulus for the word *boy* which has through previous associations become chained to *the* as a response. The word *ran* is positioned next to *boy* again because of the associations previously formed between the words, i.e., *boy* acts as a stimulus to the word *ran*. In other words, the speaker's placement of words in a sentence is based on the probability that they belong in a certain order because they have occurred in that order previously.

If this explanation of how individuals form sentences seems improbable, the reader may be assured that his skepticism is shared by many others who are interested in language. Lashly (1957), among many other theorists, cogently argued that the S–R position is not applicable to language acquisition. It remained for Chomsky, in his book *Syntactic Structures* (1957), not only to refute these theories but to offer an alternate model for language development in the form of *transformational grammar*.

Chomsky's attack on the principles of Associationism, as they were applied to language, was based primarily on the premise that they could not explain the infinite variety of sentences which humans use. He asserted that limitations of memory alone make implausible the idea that each sentence consists of chains formed through previous associations, and that a true explanation of language development must account for the generation of all linguistic elements. In short, he maintained that a body of underlying rules (grammar) must explain all linguistic production and comprehension.

Another argument against the associationist position was the fact that the probability with which one word may follow another has no bearing on whether or not a sentence is formed. Words which have a high probability of following one another, such as "Give to water flows along" do not constitute a sentence whereas words which are not commonly associated with one another such as "She delivers opinions hotly" does form a sentence. A theory of grammar which fails to differentiate between sentences and nonsense is clearly inadequate. Finally Chomsky delivered what many consider to be the coup de grace to the associationist theory, when he pointed out that a left-to-right model could not possibly explain embedding. For example, in a sentence such as "The woman who maintained that her mother was rejuvenated when she took the pill is here today," the verb *is,* according to the associationist model, should follow *woman.* The embedded words intervening between *woman* and *is* break the continuity of this relationship, and although their usage constitutes a perfectly grammatical English sentence, they clearly violate the premise that a word in a sentence is a response to the word which immediately precedes it.

In his attempts to offer a more encompassing theory of the manner in which language develops, Chomsky's principal premise has been that the rules of a grammar must account for the generation of all linguistic elements. In other words, the rules must be applicable to the production and comprehension of an infinite variety of sentences. To accomplish this, he proposed rules of formation, i.e., rules which permit the rewriting of sentences until they are reduced to their terminal elements and cannot be further simplified. For example, if we examine the sentence "The woman hit a policeman," we can call *the woman* a noun phrase and *hit a policeman* a verb phrase. The noun phrase can be rewritten as article *the* and noun *woman*, while the verb phrase can be reduced to the verb *hit*, and the noun phrase *a policeman*. The noun phrase *a policeman* can be further reduced to article *a* and noun *policeman*. At this point we have rewritten the sentence in terminal elements which cannot be further reduced.

One is left then with basic language forms which can be used to generate other sentences. In other words, the rules of formation are recursive and can be used again and again. An individual who masters this small, finite set of rules would be capable of formulating an infinite number of sentences.

Chomsky recognized certain inadequacies in rules of formation in that they do not encompass the linguistic basis for arranging terminal elements within a sentence. For example, a noun phrase such as "a policeman" in the above sentence can be transformed into the question word "whom" as in "Whom did the woman hit?" Rules of formation are not sufficient to explain the relationship between "a policeman" and "whom," although both appear to have similar roles in relation to the verb. Chomsky designated the rules required to account for this sort of linguistic relationship as *Rules of Transformation*. In our example, the transformational operation was the replacement of the noun phrase by "whom." In other words, transformation is the conversion of one linguistic structure into another by operations such as substitution ("whom" for the noun phrase), permutation (reversals of word positions such as the subject and the verb), and others. Transformational operations account for the individual's ability to form sentences in the passive voice as well as the use of negative and interrogative forms.

Of additional importance is the fact that transformational grammar reveals that surface forms of a sentence do not always completely represent all the underlying aspects which make up the sentence. Going back to our example, we note that when we transform the declarative sentence "The woman hit a policeman" into the interrogative form "Whom did the woman hit?" the auxiliary verb "did" appears. This verb would also be used if the declarative sentence were transformed to the negative form as in the sentence "The woman didn't hit a policeman." The auxiliary verb is part of the underlying or deep structure of the sentence that is not used in the particular surface structure which is a declarative sentence. This distinction between deep and surface structure of sentences constitutes one of Chomsky's major contributions to the understanding of language. Surface structure denotes the usage of particular words in a sentence, while deep structure refers to the knowledge of underlying linguistic units. The linguistic components of the deep structure account for the meaning which is to be conveyed through the rules of transformation; a variety of surface structures may be generated from a particular deep structure. Although surface structures are altered by transformations, meaning may be identical. The passive transformation, "The policeman was hit by the woman," does not alter the meaning of our example "The woman hit a policeman."

It also requires understanding of the principles of transformation to recognize that sentences which have identical surface structures according to the rules of formation have varied deep structures. For example, we can reduce a sentence such as "The woman hit the nail" to the same terminal classifications as we did with our previous sentence about the woman and the policeman. The rules for formation are identical, as are the surface structures. The variation in meaning brings us once again to an awareness of deep structure which underlies the particular surface representation of words.

The fact that the surface structure of language does not begin to convey the underlying linguistic knowledge brings us to the discussion of another of Chomsky's key tenets, i.e., the differentiation between competence and performance. Linguistic competence refers to an awareness of the underlying rules of the language which account for the relationship between semantics and phonology through syntax. This is essentially having the knowledge to relate sounds and meanings. The fact that surface structures which are uttered do not always convey the speaker's meaning is readily apparent to anyone who has ever had his statements misunderstood. It is often impossible to indicate directly in the surface structure the abstract knowledge involved in language mastery. Linguistic performance, on the other hand, refers only to that language which is produced. Another way of examining this distinction is by noting the difference between speech and language. Speech, an expressive behavior, is the act of producing meaningful sounds and is similar to linguistic performance. Language, however, is an underlying competence which the individual possesses and which is conveyed to others through speech. Chomsky's concern with the importance of this distinction centered on the fact that an individual's competence may not be reflected in his performance. Many disabilities which relate only indirectly to language, such as memory and attention, may depress language performance, while linguistic competence may be intact.

Obviously, the whole question of linguistic competence relates directly to the study of cognitive processes. The development of complex rules which determine language production is based upon underlying mentalistic behaviors. As it is not our intent to discuss in detail the relationship between cognition and language development, the reader who is interested in pursuing the topic is referred to Vygotsky (1962), Piaget (1955), Furth (1964), and Bruner (1964). Acceptance of the linguistic competence hypothesis mitigates against attributing language acquisition to environmental influences *alone* and suggests that language development, along with other types of cognitive growth, is due, to some extent, to an inherent component.

Chomsky has noted that despite the complexity of language, most children, regardless of culture or environment, have developed a sophisticated level of competence and performance before the age of five. He has attributed this capacity to the existence of a *language acquisition device* (LAD), an innate processor for linguistic rules. This is not to imply that environmental influences play no role in language acquisition. Obviously, children from different countries speak different languages. The variation in type of language they speak, however, reflects different surface structures. The capacity to master underlying rules of transformation, which are linguistic universals and applicable to all languages, is determined by the LAD.

Our synopsis of Chomsky's work, which is admittedly brief and perhaps simplistic, is probably sufficient for the reader to appreciate the extent to which his ideas are at variance with those of the S–R theorists. There is no question that his innovations revolutionized the field of psycholinguistics. His ideas provided the impetus for much research which was specific to the field of language acquisition. Many modern investigators and theoreticians, such as McNeill, Slobin, Fodor, and Menyuk, to name but a few, have expanded Chomsky's theories and are currently making important contributions to the field.

Although the vital ideas and discoveries brought forth by these individuals evoke great interest from the student of psycholinguistics, they do not appear, as yet, to have found their way in significant strength out of the universities and into the mainstream of public education. Perhaps it is the fact that advocates of transformational grammar continue to revise their theoretical positions which accounts for the lack of measurable application of this approach in the schools Possibly, too little time has passed for the evolution of instructional programs based on this particular psycholinguistic model.

It is perhaps significant that the standardized assessment tests which are based largely on a linguistic frame of reference are not widely used in the schools. Measures such as The Utah Test of Language (Mecham, Jex, and Jones 1976), Experimental Test of Comprehension as Linguistic Structure (Carrow, 1968), Northwestern Syntax Screening Test (Lee, 1969), Berko's Test of Morphology (Berko, 1958) all relate in some manner to certain aspects of Chomsky's theory; but none of them has gained a fraction of the popularity accorded the ITPA. Possibly the fact that none of these instruments begins to measure Chomsky's major constructs, i.e., deep and surface structure, performance and competence, or rules of formation and transformation, has reduced their acceptance in education. In any event, most professionals involved with the problem of assessing language recognize the urgent need for the development of a comprehensive test based on Chomsky's tenets (Rosenberg, 1971).

Summary

In this chapter we have defined psycholinguistics as the study of the mental processes which underlie the acquisition and use of language. As a relatively new discipline, it combines ideas from the fields of psychology and linguistics. The psychological theory making greatest impact in psycholinguistics today is the stimulus–response theory represented most obviously by the work of Skinner and of Osgood. The most important input from linguistics is Chomsky's postulations concerning transformational grammar. Chomsky's work was presented in an effort to caution the reader against accepting the S–R model uncritically, as well as to present an alternative method of explaining language acquisition and development.

For all practical purposes the ideas formulated by Chomsky and his associates predominate in psycholinguistics, and most modern research and theorizing reflects their influence. Interestingly, however, their concepts are not represented to a significant degree in educational programming. For example, tests of language which are based largely on their concepts are infrequently used to diagnose children's deficits. Formal instructional programs are quite rare, although a few are available.

On the other hand, although the language development models presented by Skinner and Osgood are no longer given much credibility within the discipline of psycholinguistics, their formulations are quite popular in education. Skinner's influence is not so much related to his specific explanations of language, as to his theories concerning the use of positive reinforcement techniques to strengthen all desired behaviors.

Osgood's psycholinguistic theory, however, has had an unprecedented impact on schools and clinics, undoubtedly because it is represented in the ITPA, a test which dominates the field of language measurement in the same manner that the Binet and Wechsler tests dominate the field of intellectual measurement. The vast number of research studies using the ITPA as a principal diagnostic or predictive tool attests to the interest and enthusiasm the test has evoked in education. In order to fulfill our designated task, that is to report on the educational relevancy of psycholinguistics, we must necessarily concentrate on the application of Osgoodian theory through the ITPA and its related training programs.

2

The Illinois Test of Psycholinguistic Abilities

Introduction

The principal author of the Illinois Test of Psycholinguistic Abilities (ITPA), Samuel Kirk, has on many occasions expressed his concern about the limitations of most psychometric tests used in today's schools. He notes that these indices, which are used primarily for the purposes of classification, offer little information that a teacher can use to organize a program to correct a child's particular learning problem. To help remedy this situation, he and his colleagues devised a diagnostic test which could be used to assess specific abilities and disabilities in a manner which could readily be translated into a remediation plan. In so doing he saw the need to measure a child's intraindividual differences, i.e., the variation in abilities within a single child, as opposed to his interindividual differences, i.e., the comparison of a child's performance with that of other children. His particular interest was in identifying those variables within an individual which appeared to underlie successful academic learning. Therefore, recognizing the importance of certain psycholinguistic dimensions to learning, he and his coauthors designed the ITPA, a diagnostic, intraindividual test of selected psychological and linguistic functions.

Probably the most efficient way to begin what we hope will be a thorough examination of the ITPA is to discuss the model which Kirk, McCarthy, and Kirk used to generate the subtests included in the battery. Having dealt with the theoretical bases which underlie the instrument, we will then describe each of the subtests in detail, taking special care to point out the relationship of each to the test-model. Next, we will review the literature which pertains to its reliability and validity. Finally, the diagnostic uses of the test will be examined.

The ITPA Test-Model

The model which Kirk and his colleagues employed to develop the ITPA is essentially an adaptation of the Osgood schema described in chapter 1. The reader will recall that in order to account for language behavior Osgood postulated a two-dimensional model, i.e., (1) levels of mental organization and (2) language transmission processes. Three levels of mental organization were hypothesized, including a representational (meaningful), an integrative (nonmeaningful), and a projective (reflexive) level, as well as three types of language processes, namely, decoding (receptive), associative, and encoding (expressive) processes. In the test-model presented in figure 2, the contributions of Osgood are obvious.

Though the two models are similar, there are several important differences between them. First, while remaining more or less consistent with Osgood's fundamental intentions, the names of several constructs were changed, e.g., the integration level became "the automatic level," and decoding, association, and encoding became "receptive," "organizing," and "expressive" processes. Second, the authors of the ITPA wisely chose to exclude the projective level in their test-model because they apparently believed that reflexive behaviors were not particularly amenable to learning. When one considers the improbability of successfully teaching such projective level behaviors as the involuntary knee jerk, their purposeful omission seems warranted. Third, the ITPA test-model includes memory constructs, a significant departure from the Osgoodian theory which offers no explanation regarding this function.

Fourth, the test-model's most significant departure from Osgoodian theory pertains to the addition of a third dimension—that of channel or modality. The Osgood model does not specify any particular channels of communication, as it can accommodate input and output through any combination of sensory modalities, e.g., tactile-vocal, autitory-motor, visual-vocal. Kirk, McCarthy, and Kirk arbi-

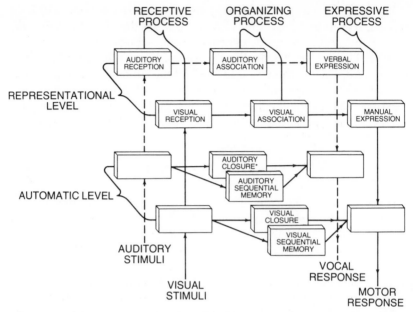

Figure 2

The ITPA Test-Model

trarily decided to measure only the auditory-vocal and the visual-motor channels since they felt these particular sensory pathways were the most critical for learning. Although their rationale might be disputed by some people, it is certainly easy to appreciate the practical necessity of preventing a test from becoming too long and cumbersome.

Each rectangle in figure 2 represents a distinct, hypothesized psycholinguistic construct, e.g., "auditory reception at the representational level." All communicative behaviors that involve primarily semantic interpretation of spoken language could be classified under this particular construct. The number of possible variations in these behaviors or tasks is almost limitless, and, of course, they are not all equally good estimates of the construct. The difficulty for the test constructors was to choose the one task which best represented the construct. Undoubtedly, this was done both deductively and empirically; whether the selection was providential, however, must depend upon the accumulation of construct validity research.

Theoretically, one could use this test-model to generate a subtest for each rectangle (i.e., construct) or even to develop a test battery comprised entirely of subtests which tap different aspects of a single construct. Kirk and his colleagues decided to design only twelve subtests, including two supplemental ones. Presumably these were selected after giving due consideration to such practical limitations as the time needed to administer the battery, the pertinence of the constructs, and the difficulty involved in test construction.

There are many individuals who feel that the ITPA is based upon an inadequate or incorrect conceptualization of language development. They maintain that since Osgood's theory of language is no longer considered plausible by most modern psycholinguists, Kirk's test-model must also be inadequate. Their logic implies that a test cannot be valid if the theory which underlies it is not valid. While this might appear correct philosophically, examination of psychometric devices, such as intelligence tests which relate most closely to school achievement, reveals little theoretical basis for their validity. Yet, they obviously have pragmatic value despite the fact that they purport to measure intelligence, a construct which has never been defined to everyone's satisfaction. Seemingly, if it can be demonstrated that the ITPA has educational relevance, the test will have value regardless of the validity of its theoretical basis.

Additionally, although modern psycholinguistic theory differs greatly from the Kirk-Osgood approach, it too consists of unproven hypotheses. The phenomenal growth and continuous change within the discipline of psycholinguistics should serve as a reminder that ideas which are enthusiastically embraced on one day are often repugnantly rejected on the next. Consequently it would appear somewhat unfair to conclude that the ITPA has no value because Osgood's conceptualizations are no longer popular.

Descriptions of ITPA Subtests

In order that the reader might more easily understand the relationship of the subtests to the test-model, we will discuss the characteristics of each construct for which a corresponding subtest was developed and will describe the format of that subtest. We must point out that many of the constructs used here are not clearly defined in the pertinent literature. Therefore, the definitions which are presented below represent our postulations of the test authors' intentions.

Representational Level Constructs and Subtests

The representational level is comprised of those communicative behaviors which involve relatively complex symbolic associations, i.e., the understanding, interpretation, and manipulation of symbols which carry meaning. For example, the task of defining a word involves the ability to make a meaningful association to a symbol such as a spoken or written word. Therefore, representational level operations include all behaviors called semantics, abstraction-categorization ability, ideation, thinking, problem solving, purposeful reading and writing, etc. The specific representational level constructs associated with the ITPA are discussed below.

A. *Receptive Processes* are the mentalistic functions involved in the recognition or comprehension of external stimuli, especially speaking, writing, and gesturing. The emphasis here is on "decoding" operations—the eliciting of those meanings related most directly to the stimulus. For example, in response to the word "dog," a child may think of his pet "Fido," barking, wagging tails, a previous experience of being bitten. These are the most "concrete" of abstractions.

   1. *Auditory Reception* is the ability to derive meaning from speech, sounds, etc. It is measured on the ITPA by having the child respond "yes" or "no" to verbal questions containing obvious absurdities, e.g., "Do ponies fly?"

   2. *Visual Reception* is the ability to gain meaning from visual symbols, including written words, sign language, pictures, or objects. To assess the construct, the child is shown a stimulus picture (e.g., of a trash can) which is quickly removed from view. He is then asked to "Find one here" from among four pictured objects, one of which is conceptually similar to the stimulus (e.g., a waste basket).

B. *Organizing Processes* are the mental abilities involved in associating incoming stimuli with previously learned information for the purpose of forming generalizations and inferences.

   These operations involve the internal manipulation of percepts and concepts and are presumed to include all abstractions, inferential thinking, and categorization abilities; for example, in response to the word "dog," the child may think "animal," "canine," "mammal."

   1. *Auditory Association* is the ability to make generalizations or inferences in response to auditory symbols, usually speech.

It is far more complex than the mere decoding of a string of spoken words; the words must "trigger" an abstraction or an idea which is only inferred in the spoken stimulus. It is measured by having the child vocally complete verbal analogies, e.g., "Bread is to eat, milk is to _____ ."

2. *Visual Association* is the ability to form generalizations, abstractions, and concepts in response to visual symbols. On the corresponding ITPA subtest, the child is asked to select a picture which most closely approximates a stimulus picture, e.g., in response to the stimulus picture cheese, he must select one of the following: bowl, spoon, cat, or mouse.

C. *Expressive Processes* are mentalistic operations which provide for the expression of ideas or other meaningful responses.

1. *Verbal Expression* is the ability to use speech to convey ideas. The construct is tapped by showing the child an object and asking him to "Tell me all about this." The score is the number of different qualities he can relate about the object pertaining to its size, color, shape, uses.etc.

2. *Manual Expression* is the ability to express ideas through movement, i.e., writing, gestures, drawing, pantomime, etc. To measure this, the child is shown a picture of an object and is asked to "Show me what you do with this."

Automatic Level Constructs and Subtests

The automatic level of mental organization involves less voluntary, nonmeaningful or nonsemantic behaviors; operations at this level are automatic, overlearned associations of highly integrated stimuli. In other words, abilities such as speed of perception, closure operations, rote memory, and phonological utterances, which require little conceptual mediation, are readily identifiable as automatic level functions.

A. *Closure Functions* — In this context, closure is represented as the ability to recognize a common phenomenon when parts are presented or the related ability to combine parts into the whole.

1. *Grammatic Closure* is the ability to use grammar proficiently, e.g., to properly use plurals, possessives, adjectives. Performance is assessed by having the child complete verbally presented sentences such as "Here is a dog, here are two_____ ."

2. *Auditory Closure* is the ability to recognize a complete auditory symbol when only part is presented. On the ITPA, it is tapped by having children supply the whole word in orally presented words, e.g., " ___ ype ___ iter." This is one of the two supplementary subtests on the battery.

3. *Sound Blending* is the ability to combine orally presented parts of words into whole words. It is measured by having the child synthesize two or more discrete sounds into a word, e.g., f _ oot. This is the second supplementary subtest.

4. *Visual Closure* is the ability to identify common objects from incomplete visual presentations. The subtest associated with this construct requires the child to locate partially hidden objects in pictures containing distracting stimuli, e.g., bottles in a kitchen scene.

B. *Sequential Memory Functions*—This is the ability to repeat immediately a sequence of nonmeaningful stimuli (i.e., direct recall).

1. *Auditory Sequential Memory* is the ability to recall correctly a series of spoken words, digits, sentences, or rhythms. The ability is assessed by having the child repeat verbally from memory sequences of digits increasing in length from two to eight. The digits are presented auditorially at a rate of two per second.

2. *Visual Sequential Memory* is the ability to recall a series of visual symbols. On this subtest, the child is shown pictures of sequences of nonmeaningful figures for a few seconds and then is asked to put chips, which have corresponding figures on them, in the same order.

The relationship of ITPA subtests to the basic Kirk clinical model is presented in table 1. Readers who desire a comprehensive listing of tests which have been "coded" in terms of Osgood's principles are referred to the appendix in Osgood and Miron (1963). A similar list of tests which is coded in the test-model's constructs is found in Myers and Hammill (1969).

As may be readily seen in table 1, six subtests at the representational level tap three processes (reception, organizing, and expression) and four channels (auditory, verbal, visual, manual). In fact, they are named according to the psycholinguistic channel and process they measure, e.g., Auditory Reception, Visual Association, etc. The authors of the test recognize the impossibility of assessing receptive and organizing abilities exclusive of any expressive component,

Table 1

*ITPA Subtests Coded
in Terms of the Test-Model*

Subtest	Level	Process	Channel
1. Auditory Reception	Representational	Reception	Auditory
2. Visual Reception	Representational	Reception	Visual
3. Auditory Association	Representational	Organizing	Auditory
4. Visual Association	Representational	Organizing	Visual
5. Verbal Expression	Representational	Expression	Verbal
6. Manual Expression	Representational	Expression	Manual
7. Visual Seq. Memory	Automatic	Organizing	Visual
8. Auditory Seq. Memory	Automatic	Organizing	Auditory/Verbal
9. Grammatic Closure	Automatic	Organizing	Auditory/Verbal
10. Visual Closure	Automatic	Organizing	Visual
11. Auditory Closure	Automatic	Organizing	Auditory/Verbal
12. Sound Blending	Automatic	Organizing	Auditory/Verbal

for naturally, an individual must make some overt motor response (e.g., speak, write, point) to indicate his proficiency. Therefore, when measuring the receptive and organizing processes, they have reduced the expressive requirements to one word or pointing responses. At this level, they are committed to measuring distinct process and channel functions and are therefore quite consistent with both the Osgood model and the Kirk adaptation.

At the automatic level, a definite departure is made in the criteria governing subtest selection, for no attempt is made to measure discretely the processes of reception or expression. Kirk and his colleagues reasoned that it is too difficult to develop subtests that assess these processes independently, i.e., which tap receptive skills without simultaneously involving expressive abilities. Instead of designing subtests of specific psychological functions, as was done at the representational level, they maintain that the subtests they have developed for the automatic level should be regarded as "whole level tests," a somewhat perplexing term. For example, one could infer from this term that each subtest taps elements of all three processes. This interpretation, however, would be contradicted by inspection of the channel dimension in table 1 since Visual Closure and Visual Sequential Memory appear to us to be measures of receptive processes. They primarily involve visual input. The expressive or manual output requirements are quite minimal, i.e., pointing and simple manipulation respectively. Therefore, the implication that all three processes are incorporated in each of the automatic level subtests is unsubstantiated.

Confusion concerning the conceptualization of the automatic level is confounded further by the test authors' apparent intention that these "whole level" subtests should be considered to be measures of organizing processes (see figure 2), where these tests are actually illustrated graphically under the heading "Organizing Process." If this is indeed their intention, the rationale underlying the construct "organizing process" would differ dramatically between levels. We believe it does and should. For example, at the representational level, the test authors have attempted to minimize the receptive and expressive components to the point where organizing ability (i.e., abstraction, inferential thinking, reasoning, etc.) can be assessed relatively independent of them, an effort consistent with Osgood's schema. At the automatic level, where these high level abilities theoretically do not exist, the nature of the organizing processes must be viewed differently.

The only reasonable explanation of which we can conceive is to consider organizing processes at this level to include only those tasks which associate receptive and expressive functions, a position which we suggest is not too inconsistent with Osgood's basic premises. Thus, Auditory Sequential Memory, which requires the child to attend to digits and to repeat them—in fact all tasks of reproduction —could be considered as measures of some organizing process. Applying this definition to the ITPA automatic level subtests, we note that once again Visual Closure and possibly Visual Sequential Memory do not meet the requirement of cross-receptive/expressive process. For these reasons, we remain confused about the theoretical foundations of the automatic level of the ITPA.

Unlike the representational level where subtests measure discrete psycholinguistic functions on two dimensions, the test authors have chosen to create six subtests, two of which are supplemental, at the automatic level in order to assess different aspects of closure or memory. The only psycholinguistic dimension upon which these tests vary is that of channel. For example, four of the subtests tap auditory-verbal facility and two deal with visual skill (see table 1). To include tests which appear to be conceptually identical, in terms of the generating model, in a battery which is represented to measure specific psycholinguistic abilities seems somewhat inconsistent and inefficient. Perhaps, although the authors do not state it, the primary consideration in developing subtests at the automatic level is content, a decision which apparently represents another departure from the original purpose in developing the test, i.e., to provide a measure of specific psycholinguistic abilities.

Diagnostic Uses of the ITPA

The ITPA is designed for use with children between the ages of two and ten who are demonstrating certain learning problems. For example, it might be administered to a child who is having difficulty in reading or speaking. The rationale underlying its use is that it is desirable to identify deficits in abilities presumed to be correlates of reading in order to provide the correct approach for remediation.

Once the test is administered, the examiner must interpret the data gathered in the most useful manner possible. The ITPA is devised to permit an intraindividual approach to diagnosis, in that a child's performance on each subtest is compared with his general performance in order to reveal discrepancies in the child's own growth. Comparison of a child's performance with that of other children the same age is not necessarily part of this approach, although it is possible to interpret ITPA scores in this manner. By comparing a child's performance on each of the subtests with his general performance on the test, his particular strengths and weaknesses become apparent. This type of evaluation would lead to the prescription of specific remedial activities.

Through the use of tables provided in the test manual, the examiner can convert raw score to scaled scores and psycholinguistic ages. The composite psycholinguistic age is a global score representing the sum of the raw scores. It gives a general index of the level of psycholinguistic functioning in years and months. As an age score it can be compared conveniently to other educational indices which are scored in a similar manner. Because this score does not consider variance, however, it should not be used to make across-age comparisons. The most efficient method of analyzing test results is through scaled scores. These indices are based on both mean performances and variability about the mean. Consequently they are appropriately used for comparison of all age levels. Because of the increased interpretability of these scores, the test authors recommend that they be plotted on test profiles.

We can demonstrate the point best by reproducing the Summary Sheet and Profile of Abilities which are part of every test protocol. The subject is an eight-year-old, underachieving male, and his scores are recorded in figure 3.

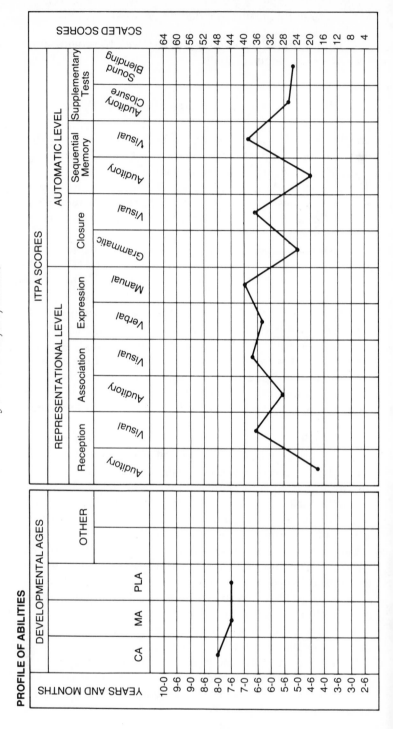

Figure 3
ITPA Summary Sheet and Profile of Abilities

Summary Sheet

SUBTEST	REPRESENTATIONAL LEVEL — AUDITORY-VOCAL Raw Score	Age Score	Scaled Score	REPRESENTATIONAL LEVEL — VISUAL-MOTOR Raw Score	Age Score	Scaled Score	AUTOMATIC LEVEL — AUDITORY-VOCAL Raw Score	Age Score	Scaled Score	AUTOMATIC LEVEL — VISUAL-MOTOR Raw Score	Age Score	Scaled Score
AUDITORY RECEPTION	14	4-1	18									
VISUAL RECEPTION				26	8-4	37						
VISUAL MEMORY										22	8-4	38
AUDITORY ASSOCIATION	24	6-9	29									
AUDITORY MEMORY							8	3-0	20			
VISUAL ASSOCIATION				27	8-5	38						
VISUAL CLOSURE										28	8-3	37
VERBAL EXPRESSION	30	7-8	35									
GRAMMATIC CLOSURE							17	6-0	24			
MANUAL EXPRESSION				30	9-10	40						
(Supplementary tests) AUDITORY CLOSURE							17	5-9	27			
SOUND BLENDING							9	5-3	26			

SUMMARY SCORES:

Sum of Raw Scores: **226**

Composite PLA: **6-9**

Sum of SS: **316**

Mean SS: **31.6**

Median SS: **36**

31

It is clear, from examining the summary sheet, that this particular child's visual-motor skills are superior to his auditory-vocal ability at both the representational and automatic levels. The Profile of Abilities graph shows that his performances on the Auditory Reception and Auditory Sequential Memory subtests were particularly weak, as he has scored approximately four years below the expected level for an eight-year-old.

What precisely has the test revealed about this child? It is known that he did poorly when material was presented orally and that he had particular difficulty when he had to identify verbal absurdities (Auditory Reception) and repeat digits in sequence (Auditory Sequential Memory). His profile resembles that of a child with a hearing deficit and this premise warrants further investigation. Based on this profile, however, it is not appropriate to assume that this child is weak in auditory sequential memory and auditory reception when these terms are used generically. Even if it is granted that Kirk's conceptualizations are accurate labels of discrete mental processes, the reader must keep in mind that the tasks in the ITPA which measure these constructs represent only one aspect of each of these phenomena. It is possible to measure auditory memory in any manner of ways, even by asking a child to state his name. There is no reason to assume that he would do poorly on other tests of auditory memory. The test authors make it quite clear that the results alone should not be used to make overall conclusions about any individual. They recommend that it be used to demonstrate areas of weaknesses which should then be investigated through further formalized testing, informal or criterion-referenced testing, and general observation.

Kirk and Kirk (1971) also point out that although the ITPA and several other tests might disclose specific weaknesses, remediation should not be restricted to those particular abilities, but should be broad enough to include many related skills. In other words, our subject's teacher should not attempt to train only auditory memory skills and auditory receptive activities but should supply the child with many related educational activities. The Kirk and Kirk book, *Psycholinguistic Learning Disabilities,* is replete with many suggestions for providing such remediation.

Reliability

Any test which is to be effective as a measure of the abilities of individual children must have a high reliability. This is especially important in tests like the ITPA because in these instances a child's test performance can result in the preparation of a lengthy instructional prescription, which can commit his teacher to a considerable expenditure of time and materials. The reliability of the ITPA has been the subject of a modest amount of study. In particular, its internal consistency, stability, and standard error of measurement have been investigated.

Sedlak and Weener (1973) maintain that "estimates of reliability are influenced by the variability in the sample on which they are based. If the test is used to make distinctions between students within a grade, age, or ability level, the reliability coefficients should be based solely on that grade, age, or ability level, and not on a wider range of abilities"; studies which use a heterogeneous sample "may have only limited generalizability" (p. 116). Hubschmann, Polizzotto, and Kaliski (1970), Wisland and Many (1967), Hatch and French (1971), and Paraskevopoulos and Kirk (1969) have all studied the reliability of the ITPA. As only the Paraskevopoulos and Kirk study is consistent with the suggestions of Sedlak and Weener with which we agree the discussions which follow rest mainly on its findings.

Internal Consistency

Internal consistency reflects the homogeniety of items within a test, i.e., the extent to which each item measures the same function. In the case of the ITPA, each subtest is designed to assess a discrete and independent ability; therefore, the homogeniety of the items within each subtest is particularly pertinent. If, for example, the items of the Auditory Reception subtest are not highly intercorrelated, it would mean that to a disturbing degree the items measure a construct other than auditory reception. One might then question whether the test could be used as the basis for making diagnostic statements about that construct.

Paraskevopoulos and Kirk (1969) used data gathered from 962 children in the ITPA standardization sample to compute internal consistency reliability coefficients. Because of the nature of the subtests' format, two different techniques had to be used—Kuder-Richardson, #20, and Hoyt's analysis of variance procedure. Accepting .80 as the criterion of adequate reliability for diagnostic devices, one may conclude that, with the single exception of Visual Closure and possibly of Visual Sequential Memory, the subtests of the ITPA evidenced acceptable internal consistency at all age levels. Apparently, those persons who use the ITPA diagnostically can feel reasonably confident that most of the subtests have homogeneous items.

Stability Reliability

The importance of stability reliability is obvious—for of what value is knowledge of a child's test score, if it varies widely on a day-to-day basis? For example, it would be most embarrassing to examine a child on one day, diagnose his psycholinguistic difficulties, recommend a remedial program to his teacher, and then to retest him on the very next day and find no indication of his "previously diagnosed" problem.

Stability reliability involves the extent to which test scores remain stable over time and is measured by the test-retest procedure. Paraskevopoulos and Kirk (1969) provided information on 198 four-, six-, and eight-year-old children from the standardization sample. Their results would suggest that only Auditory Association and Auditory Sequential Memory have adequate stability. However, we maintain that their study should not be taken as definitive because the five-month time lapse between the test and the retest was too long; two weeks or a month would have been more desirable. Therefore, we are inclined to accept their explanation of the resultant low coefficients. They suggest that due to the developmental nature of psycholinguistic abilities and to the influence of ongoing educational and remedial programs in the schools, marked change in test performance should be expected; and, as a consequence, stability coefficients should not be evaluated in the same manner as those obtained on a test of a fixed product. In other words, the .80 criterion is in such cases unduly rigorous. This is a valid position provided that enough time has passed for remediation and/or development to have occurred. In any event, the test-retest reliability of the ITPA is an area in need of more study.

Standard Error of Measurement

Standard error of measurement reflects consistency of performance in that it shows the extent of deviation due to error for each obtained score; in other words, it establishes the zone within which the true score lies. A test with high reliability coefficients usually has a small standard error of measurement.

SEm is an important statistic for any test which attempts to compile a diagnostic profile based on comparisons of specific subtest performances. The larger the SEm band around each score, the greater the possibility that what appears to be a deficit in performance is simply a statistical artifact due to chance. Paraskevopoulos and Kirk (1969) have computed SEm's for raw, psycholinguistic age, and scaled scores on data from the standardization sample and have provided several tables for ITPA users to consult in order to obtain this information for any aged child. Subtest SEm's for scaled scores, the most useful indices of performance, do not exceed 4.5 for any age level. Visual Closure has consistently high SEm's whereas those computed for Auditory Reception are generally low. There is relative consistency for all age levels.

As long as SEm is taken into consideration, comparison of scaled scores in profile analysis is useful to the diagnostician. The temptation to regard each subtest score as a fixed point and to ignore error variance might be avoided by plotting the SEm zone around each score. This type of graphic depiction would clearly demonstrate whether score differences were extreme enough to be true indices of psycholinguistic deficiency.

To conclude, Paraskevopoulos and Kirk are to be credited with providing the reader with a thorough examination of the ITPA's reliability. On the basis of their findings, one may conclude that the internal consistency of the subtests is adequate for diagnostic purposes. Their information pertaining to the stability of the scores is inconclusive. While hundreds of studies have used the ITPA, it is unfortunate that only Paraskevopoulos and Kirk have studied the reliability of the instrument at specific age levels, a major criterion for adequate reliability research. Replication of their procedures on both typical and various groups of exceptional children is still necessary.

Validity

"In crudest terms," says Guilford (1956), "we may say that a test is valid when it measures what it is presumed to measure" (p. 461). In a test which presumes to measure twelve discrete mental functions for the purpose of identifying a child's strengths and weaknesses, questions of validity assume unusual importance. Particularly relevant to the ITPA are construct validity, predictive and concurrent validity, and diagnostic validity.

Construct Validity

Construct validity is perhaps the most important type of validity since it concerns the degree to which the underlying traits of a test can be identified and the extent to which these traits reflect the theoretical model on which the test is based. With regard to the ITPA, construct validity involves determining the extent to which each subject represents a discrete psycholinguistic ability as depicted on the test-model.

The significance of this type of validity is overriding, for the ITPA may only appear to reflect the test-model by using similar terminology. It may, in fact, be nothing more than a composite of twelve measures of specific content which bear no fundamental relationship to the test-model or psycholinquistics. There is little reason to accept as fact the test authors' assertion that a subtest, such as Auditory Sequential Memory (a test of short-term memory for digits presented orally), is a representation of the psycholinguistic variables automatic level, auditory channel, and organizing process. The validity of this assertion must be demonstrated experimentally.

The usual method for investigating construct validity is factor analysis, a useful statistical technique for revealing underlying traits. In this procedure variables which are most alike cluster together on common factors. Using factor analysis, many attempts have been made to study the basic constructs of the ITPA. On the whole, these investigations have produced conflicting, uninterpretable results, probably because their authors did not include in their analysis "true" criterion-referenced tests, i.e., tests which were especially selected to measure the same dimensions as the ITPA.

In some cases the subtests of the ITPA were factor analyzed without any criterion tests, a treatment which maximized their intercorrelations and resulted in multiple subtest loadings on large general factors (Leventhal and Stedman, 1970; Mittler and Ward, 1970; Ryckman and Wiegerink, 1969; Semmel and Mueller, 1965; Wisland and Many, 1969; Burns, 1973). These results were generally interpreted as indicating that ITPA subtests were interdependent and consequently measured a general linguistic ability rather than the twelve discrete skills postulated by Kirk, McCarthy, and Kirk. Such conclusions may mistakenly imply a lack of construct validity.

Other studies combined the ITPA with standardized tests bearing little theoretical relationship to the subtests, e.g., tests of intelligence, readiness, or school achievement (Haring and Ridgway, 1967; Horner, 1967; Leton, 1972; Ryckman, 1967; Smith and Marx, 1971). Factors which emerged from these studies merely reflected the criterion variables which had been used. None of this research has uncovered reliable information regarding the fundamental construct validity of the ITPA.

In only two studies, Newcomer, Hare, Hammill, and McGettigan (1975) and Hare, Hammill, and Bartel (1973) was the construct validity of the ITPA investigated using criterion tests which were specifically designed to parallel the functions supposedly measured by the ITPA subtests. The work of Hare, Hammill, and Bartel dealt with six subtests and essentially confirmed their construct validity. Newcomer et al. matched all twelve ITPA subtests with two types of criterion measures: tests which met each specification of the test-model but differed in content and tests in which content and the psycholinguistic dimensions of level and process were held constant while channel was varied.

Using this approach, the construct validity of each ITPA subtest was determined by the extent to which it "loaded" on a factor populated by criterion tests of identical psycholinguistic qualities. For example, the ITPA subtest Auditory Sequential Memory, which is coded in psycholinguistic terms as auditory channel, organizing process, and automatic level, would be expected to load independently of all other ITPA subtests and load with criterion tests which also measure auditory, organizing, and automatic dimensions. Conclusions and implications drawn from predictive or concurrent studies regarding various mentalistic variables, i.e., auditory processing, visual processing, receptive ability, etc., are meaningless if the test cannot, in fact, be shown to measure these functions.

On the whole, the results of the Newcomer et al. study are clearly supportive of the assumption of Kirk, McCarthy, and Kirk that the ITPA measures discrete psycholinguistic variables, at least when administered to normal fourth grade children. In addition, the subtests apparently do represent at least two of the three constructs which theoretically underlie the test. Level of organization and process were largely substantiated. The validity of the ITPA subtests regarding independence, channel process, and level are summarized in table 2.

Any weakness regarding the construct validity of the ITPA subtests appears primarily due to the modality dimension. Except for the Visual Closure subtest, the visual channel is completely without substantiation as a valid dimension. Both the Visual Association and Visual Reception subtests factored with auditory tasks and therefore could not be considered as valid for channel. The Visual Sequential Memory subtest appears totally lacking in construct validity, i.e., not valid on all three dimensions. The auditory channel has greater credibility but may lack the degree of validity necessary to form conclusions

Table 2

ITPA Subtest Independence and Reflection of
Three Psycholinguistic Constructs

ITPA Subtests	Independence	Channel	Constructs* Process	Level
Auditory Association	Yes	Yes	Yes	Yes
Verbal Expression	Yes	Yes	Yes	Yes
Visual Association	Yes	No	Yes	Yes
Manual Expression	Yes	No	Yes	Yes
Auditory Reception	No	Possible	Yes	Yes
Visual Reception	No	No	Yes	Yes
Auditory Sequential Memory	Yes	Yes	Yes	Yes
Visual Closure	Yes	Yes	Yes	Yes
Grammatic Closure	Yes	Possible	Possible	Possible
Auditory Closure	Yes	Possible	Possible	Possible
Sound Blending	Yes	Possible	Possible	Possible
Visual Sequential Memory	No	No	No	No

Constructs:
Channel = Involves auditory, visual, vocal, or motor modalities
Process = Either reception, organizing, or expression
Level   = Either representation or automatic (integrative)

about individual behavior. Although the integrity of the auditory channel appears established for the Auditory Association, Auditory Sequential Memory, and Verbal Expression subtests, there is some question concerning Grammatic Closure, Auditory Reception, Sound Blending, and Auditory Closure. Further empirical evidence is required before the full value of the auditory subtests can be determined.

With the exception of the channel dimension, the ITPA can be regarded as a valid representative of the constructs of the test-model and to some extent of the Osgood model as well. For the most part, the subtests are discrete measures and do not tap the same constructs. The dimensions of level, i.e., representative and automatic, were proved to be different and the separation of three processes (reception, organization, and expression) was established. Despite the "wash out" of modality this conclusion makes investigations of concurrent, predictive, and diagnostic relationships much more interesting. The relationships between ITPA subtests and academic achievement, for example, may be interpreted as depicting the influence of various psycholinguistic abilities on school learning, not simply the inexplicable correlations between tests of undefined validity.

Concurrent Validity

Concurrent validity is concerned with comparing a test with existing criteria; e.g., a language test might be correlated with oral communication ability as measured by teachers' ratings. A considerable number of pertinent concurrent validity studies have accumulated. For the most part, these all deal with the relationship of the ITPA subtests to measures of academic achievement, intellectual ability, linguistic performance, perceptual-motor proficiency, etc.

McCarthy and Olson (1964) correlated each subtest with a different criterion test with which they assumed the subtest shared a theoretical relationship. All the resultant r's were statistically significant, though those associated with Visual Reception, Auditory Reception, Visual Association, Verbal Expression, and Visual Sequential Memory were lower than .35. One might argue that the concurrent validity of these tests was not demonstrated by their research. Horner (1967) studied the relationship of the ITPA to the Parsons Language Sample, a language test based on the postulations of Skinner, and found considerable support for all subtests. Washington and Teska (1970), Weaver and Weaver (1967), Milgram (1967), Giebink and Marden (1968), and many others have investigated the relationship of the ITPA to various measures of intelligence with generally supportive results. Two particularly interesting sources of information on this topic are Sedlak and Weener (1973), and Proger, Cross, and Berger (1973), who present a synthesis of the existing validity research.

While the ITPA has been correlated repeatedly with psychoeducational variables, the validity of the test as a measure of language is relatively unexplored. It is indeed surprising that the most obvious approach to validation, i.e., the correlation of the ITPA with tests like the Northwestern Syntax Screening Test, the Berko Test of Morphology, the Utah Test of Language, and the Experimental Test of Comprehension as Linguistic Structure, seems to have been almost completely avoided.

Studies pertaining to the validity of the ITPA as a predictor of academic achievement have been singled out and are dealt with separately in chapter 3 because of their importance to school programming.

Diagnostic Validity

Diagnostic validity in a test is evidenced when groups of children, who have known abilities or disabilities, perform in a way which is consistent, i.e., predictable, in terms of the test's constructs. For example, if the ITPA does measure auditory and visual processing, then the performance of a group of auditory aphasics should differ in a predictable manner from a group of legally blind children, which is the case (Olson, 1961; Bateman, 1963). The aphasics do well on the visual subtests and poorly on the auditory subtests; the blind children do the reverse. Groups of receptive auditory aphasics and hard-of-hearing children might be expected to display similar test profiles, which they do (Reichstein, 1963). In similar fashion, Myers (1965) tested ITPA diagnostic validity in discriminating between the performance of spastic and athetoid cerebral palsied children. She predicted differences between groups at the automatic level and inferior performances for both groups when compared to normals. This proved to be the case. The literature is replete with similar studies. Although in some cases they involve samples of children so severely handicapped, as with the blind and deaf groups, that the results appear to do little more than demonstrate the obvious, most evoke more subtle diagnostic discriminations. In many instances, they involve comparison of psycholinguistic patterns of handicapped children with those of children considered normal. The pertinent characteristics of many of these studies are presented in table 3. The findings of these investigations are summarized below.

Handicapped Learners.   In many cases, authors found that handicapped learners scored below normal in almost all areas tapped by the ITPA. For example, the children with articulation disorders studied by Ferrier (1966), Hallom (1964), and Foster (1963) fell below standardization norms on all subtests but Visual Reception. They had particular difficulty with all subtests at the automatic level. Jorstad (1971) and Smith (1970) obtained similar results with groups of learning disabled children. Retardates also performed in a generally depressed manner and showed significant weakness on the auditory-vocal subtests at the automatic level (Bilovsky and Share, 1965; McCarthy, 1965; Mueller, 1964; Bateman and Wetherell, 1965; Brown and Rice, 1968).

Table 3

Research Relating to Diagnostic Validity
(i.e., Group Differentiation)

Author(s)	Edition	Number of Subjects	Types of Subjects	Results
Barritt, Semmel & Weener (1966)	Experimental	191	Educational Deprived & Advantaged	Advantaged superior on all auditory tests
Bilovsky & Share (1965)	Experimental	30	Mongoloid	Significantly weak in Auditory-vocal Automatic and Auditory-Sequencing
Brown & Rice (1967)	Experimental	50	EMR	Deficiencies at Automatic-Sequential level
Butts (1970)	Revised	48	Lower & Middle class Black & White	Whites superior on all tasks
Caccamo & Yater (1972)	Revised	22	Blacks, Down's Syndrome	Handicapped blacks do not show the psycholinguistic patterns attributed to normal blacks
Cicerelli, Granger, Schemmel, Cooper, & Holthouse (1971)	Revised	1495	Lower Class, Blacks & Whites & Mexican American	Whites high in Auditory Reception, Auditory Association & Grammatic Closure. Blacks high in Auditory Sequential Memory. M.A. high in Visual Sequential Memory
Ferrier (1966)	Experimental	40	Functional Speech Disorder	Poor on Automatic-Sequential
Foster (1963)	Experimental	30	Articulation Disorder	Poor on Automatic-Sequential
Glovsky (1970)	Revised	24	MR aphasic and non-aphasic	Non-Aphasic were superior in auditory vocal areas
Hallom (1964)	Experimental	25	Functional Speech Disorder	Depressed profiles, Poorest on Automatic-Sequential tests
Jorstad (1971)	Revised	20	Mexican Americans	Significantly poor on all Auditory tests
Kuski (1969)	Revised	150	EMR & Normal Sioux EMR Whites	Normal Sioux better on Sound Blending. All S's below normal

(Continued)

Table 3 (cont'd.)

Author(s)	Edition	Number of Subjects	Types of Subjects	Results
Lombardi (1970)	Revised	80	Papago Indians	Significantly below norms on all tests but Visual Sequential Memory
McCarron (1971)	Revised	150	Culturally Deprived, White, Black, Mexican	Mexican Americans & blacks weak in Grammatic Closure & Auditory Association
McCarthy (1965)	Experimental	30	Mongoloid	Significantly weak in Auditory-vocal Automatic and Auditory Association
Mittler & Ward (1970)	Experimental	96	Upper & Lower Class	Auditory-vocal tests affected most by SES
Mueller (1964)	Experimental	63	Gifted, EMR, TMR	Gifted were superior on all subtests
Mueller & Weaver (1964)	Experimental	80	Institutionalized & Non-institutionalized TMR	Institutionalized were superior on Auditory-Vocal Automatic and Auditory-Vocal Sequencing
Paraskevopoulos & Kirk (1969)	Revised	245	3 Social Classes	Significant correlations between social class and Auditory Reception, Auditory Association, Verbal Expression, Grammatic Closure & Visual Closure
Smith (1970)	Revised	20	Educational Handicapped	Below norms on all tests but Sound Blending, Visual Reception, Manual Expression & Auditory Sequential Memory
Smith & McWilliams (1968)	Experimental	136	Cleft Palate	Poorest on Vocal & Motor Expression
Stephenson & Gay (1972)	Revised		Lower & Middle Class Black & White	Performance of whites, not blacks, is influenced by SES. Blacks and low SES show more variability
Teasdale & Katz (1968)	Experimental		Upper & Lower class	Auditory-vocal tests affected most by SES
Webb (1968)	Revised	60	Lower class Anglo, Latin American & Black	Latin Americans & blacks deficient on Auditory-Vocal and strong on Visual-Motor subjects

42

Social Classes.　Studies involving the use of the ITPA with children of various social classes have uncovered certain performance patterns. Children with middle class status typically function better on auditory subtests (Paraskevopoulos and Kirk, 1968; Mittler and Ward, 1970; Teasdale and Katz, 1968; Butts, 1970; Stephenson and Gay, 1972).

Ethnic Groups.　Investigations conducted among various ethnic groups also appear to demonstrate certain predictable psycholinguistic patterns. The reader should note, however, that the uncontrolled effect of social class in many of these studies may confound these conclusions. In other words, it is difficult to know if differences obtained are due to the effects of class or ethnic group. For example, blacks and Mexican-American children frequently appear to do less well than Anglo-Americans on auditory subtests. However, the samples of black and Mexican-American children are usually drawn from lower socioeconomic groups (McCarron, 1971; Webb, 1968; Barritt, Semmel, and Weener, 1966). Cicerelli, Granger, Schemmel, Cooper, and Holthouse (1971), using an unusually large number of subjects who were part of the Head Start program, found that blacks do best on Auditory Sequential Memory, Mexicans on Visual Sequential Memory, and Anglo-Americans on Grammatic Closure, Auditory Reception, and Auditory Association.

It seems unwarranted to assume that diagnostic validity established for groups is applicable to individual cases. For example, even through general deficits at the automatic level are characteristic of retarded educable children as a group, this performance pattern is not always demonstrated by individual retardates. Group results, as a matter of course, mask the performances of individuals.

Generally speaking, the principal ITPA author, S. Kirk, has made an extensive effort to present adequate normative data regarding the test (Paraskevopoulos and Kirk, 1969). Kirk and Kirk (1971) also have provided many guidelines for its use and interpretation. Although test users are benefited by this type of information, its availability does not insure the educational importance of the test. Regardless of how proficiently a test is administered and interpreted, it is not really helpful to teachers unless it relates closely to academic achievement. Since educational significance of the test is so important, it will be discussed in detail in chapters 3 and 4.

3

Educational Significance of the ITPA

Introduction

The principal value of any assessment device that is used in the schools depends upon the extent to which it relates to academic achievement. No matter how astutely designed, accurately standardized, or brilliantly conceptualized a test may be, it is relatively worthless to educators unless its results can be used to improve children's capacity to perform such basic school activities as reading, spelling, and arithmetic. In other words, it must be demonstrated that a test has educational significance.

The widespread use of the ITPA with children who experience academic problems suggests that many educators and psychologists have accepted as valid the premise that the ITPA is an educationally significant test. When a slow learning or underachieving child also shows deficiencies on the ITPA subtests, many educators appear confident in assuming that the psycholinguistic deficits are causing or contributing to a pupil's academic difficulties in some way. As a result they frequently use information derived from the ITPA as a basis for prescribing specific remedial activities designed to remove "blocks" to learning and/or to increase academic competence. Apparently, the equally probable supposition that a child might evidence both an academic and a psycholinguistic problem which are totally un-related to each other is given little credence.

Because we consider it of critical importance to validate the as-sumption that the ITPA has educational significance, we will provide the reader with as much empirical evidence relevant to this question as we have been able to find.

In order to do this, the literature which deals with two types of investigative approaches will be reviewed. One method, correlative study, involves testing groups of children on the ITPA and various academic variables and correlating the scores in order to determine the predictive relationship between the tests. The other approach involves identifying groups of children who differ in academic com-petence (such as good and poor readers) and measuring the extent to which they also differ in psycholinguistic ability; this procedure estab-lishes a test's diagnostic validity for academic competencies. In addi-tion to the reviews of the existent research, the results of a study which employed both the correlative and the diagnostic-group differ-ence techniques with the same sample of children will be discussed in detail.

If the evidence indicates that the correlative and diagnostic rela-tionships between the ITPA and academic achievement indices are inconsequential, it would signify that the test lacks educational rele-vance and would suggest that educators should reject the assumption that the ITPA skills constitute important requisites for academic achievement. It would further imply that the extensive use of the instrument for educational diagnosis and remedial planning would be largely unwarranted. On the other hand, data which indicates that the ITPA subtests are indeed highly related to academic skills would in part support the diagnostic value of the ITPA as the basis for preparing individualized programs in psycholinguistics for particular children.

Review of Correlational Research

Correlation is a statistical procedure which measures the relation-ship among variables. Educators can use it to estimate a child's per-formance on one test using the knowledge of his performance on another test as the basis for the prediction. Use of correlation in this manner establishes a test's predictive validity. For example, relatively high positive correlations between the ITPA and the Metropolitan

Achievement Tests would indicate that children who do well on the ITPA also do well on the MAT. This would also suggest that the ITPA has predictive validity for the academic skills measured on the MAT, i.e., reading, arithmetic, spelling, etc.

The reader should note that the demonstration of significant relationships between the ITPA subtests and various academic indices would not necessarily mean that school achievement is predicated on the development of the abilities measured by the ITPA, for correlation does not indicate the direction of a relationship, nor does it imply cause and effect. It is quite possible that academic and psycholinguistic abilities are mutually dependent on a multitude of extraneous variables, such as intelligence, self-concept, learning opportunities, social class, and age. For example, in a four-year-old child vocabulary development and motor ability might appear to be highly related when in fact they are both strongly dependent on chronological age. As the child grows older, commensurate improvement occurs in both variables; but increased motor efficiency will not necessarily affect vocabulary acquisition, nor will the mastery of more word meanings result in increased dexterity. Therefore, conclusive evidence of the existence of significant correlations between the ITPA subtests and academic measures would be an essential first step in investigating the nature of the relationship. On the other hand, failure to obtain significant correlations between the ITPA and academic achievement measures would suggest that since no underlying relationship exists, further speculation or investigation into the instructional usefulness of the ITPA would be superfluous.

As to the magnitude of the correlations necessary to constitute a substantial relationship, Guilford (1956) has suggested that correlation coefficients of .3 or greater are minimally acceptable for predictive validity purposes. He regards coefficients falling below this figure as small (.2 to .29) or negligible (less than .2). However, Garrett (1954) cautions that only coefficients of .4 or above are useful. Caught between experts, we have compromised and chosen .35 to serve as the cut-off point between coefficients with predictive usefulness and those without.

Two types of correlative research are reviewed in this chapter: concurrent studies and longitudinal studies. Concurrent studies are those in which the scores on the ITPA and achievement tests are obtained at approximately the same time. Longitudinal studies are those in which ITPA results are correlated with achievement indices that are obtained after a lapse of time.

An important dimension in this review of the correlation literature is the particular consideration given to those studies which attempt to control for the effects of mental age or intelligence on the variables in question. As there is a substantial correlation between mental ability and both psycholinguistic and academic tests, any significant correlation between psycholinguistic and academic skills might reflect their mutual relationship with intelligence rather than to each other.

An overview of the correlative research reviewed is presented in table 4. A total of twenty-eight studies are included—twenty-four reported short-term relationships and four reported longitudinal relationships. Among the short-term studies, six partialled out the influence of intelligence. In all, a total of 1360 relevant correlation coefficients are reported. Most of these studies involve "normal" children between the ages of six and nine who were enrolled in the primary grades. Academic achievement was most frequently measured by the Wide Range Achievement Test, California Achievement Test, Metropolitan Achievement Test, SRA Achievement Series, and the Diagnostic Reading Scale.

Concurrent Research

The twenty-four studies which dealt with the concurrent relationship between the ITPA and various academic achievement tests yielded 1152 correlation coefficients. Considered independently these coefficients are so remarkably disparate that they preclude the formation of accurate conclusions relevant to the relationship of any of the ITPA subtests to the achievement criteria. A fair index of the consensus of the results can be obtained by examining median coefficients for each of the ITPA subtests and specific areas of academic achievement, i.e., reading, spelling, and arithmetic. The median coefficients are presented in table 5. This composite approach also eliminates the temptation to fixate on the findings of an individual study while excluding consideration of equally good research which might offer contrary conclusions.

The ITPA and Reading.   Most of the studies reviewed investigated the relationship between the ITPA and reading. A total of 820 correlation coefficients depicting this relationship were reported. Only three subtests, Auditory Association, Grammatic Closure, and Sound Blending, as well as the Composite Score, established median coefficients which reached or exceeded .35. The other subtests including all those measuring visual processing skills yielded coefficients which are either not statistically significant at the .05 level or are so low as to

Table 4

Characteristics of ITPA Correlational Studies

Author	Date	Number of Subjects	Ages	Type of Subjects	Longitudinal	IQ Control	Number of Coefficients	Reading	Spelling	Arithmetic
Bannatyne & Wichiarajote	1969	50	8	Normal	No	No	4	—	IST	—
Bruininks	1969	105	8	Disadvantaged	No	Yes	2	MAT	—	—
Dillon	1966	50	7–11	Cerebral Palsy Normal	No	No	60	IRI/GATES	—	—
Egeland, DiNello & Carr	1970	82	6 & 8	Males	Yes	No	36	MAT	MAT	—
Elkins	1973	97	7–8	Normal	No	No	60	IRI	—	—
Golden & Steiner	1969	20	7	Normal	No	No	15	GATES	—	—
Goodstein, Whitney & Cawley	1970	108	7	Disadvantaged	No	No	9	SRA	—	—
Guest	1971	47	6	Normal	No	No	55	SAT	SAT	SAT
Guthrie & Goldberg	1972	124	8–10	Reading Problems	No	Yes	6	WRAT/GRAY/MAT	—	—
Hammill, Larsen, Parker, Bagley & Sanford	1974	48	6	Normal	No	Yes	9	MAT	—	—
Hammill, Parker & Newcomer	1975	137	9	Normal	No	Yes	36	CAT	CAT	CAT
Haring & Ridgeway	1967	106	6	Normal	No	No	54	WRAT	—	—
Hirshoren	1969	40	5–7	Normal	Yes	No	45	CAT	CAT	CAT
Ikeda	1971	50	8	Normal	No	Yes	26	GATES	—	—
Kiniry	1972	60	6–10	Normal/LD	No	No	96	WRAT/GATES	WRAT	WRAT

	Year	N	Grade	Classification			N			
McCarthy & Olson	1964	86	7–8	Normal	No	No	8	DRS/SAT	—	—
Mueller	1965	89	6–8	EMR	No	No	12	CAT/WRAT	CAT/WRAT	CAT/WRAT
Mueller	1969	89	8 10	EMR	Yes	No	12	NYAT/WRAT	NYAT/WRAT	NYAT/WRAT
Rosenfield	1971	30	6	Normal	No	No	26	DRS	—	—
Sabatino & Hayden	1970	252 220	6–9 9–11	"Failing"	No	No	12	Gil./WRAT	—	WRAT
Serwer & Badian	No Date	55	5–6	"High Risk"	No	No	48	MAT	MAT	—
Sowell & Larsen	1974	88	8–10	LD	No	No	12	SAT	—	—
Sumner	1966	50	10–14	EMR	No	Yes	9	DRS	—	—
Warden	1967	67	5–6	Normal	No	No	50	CAT	CAT	CAT
Washington & Teska	1970	996	5–7	Normal	No	No	160	CAT/WRAT	CAT/WRAT	CAT/WRAT
Westinghouse Learning Corp.	1969	986	7–9	Disadvantaged	Yes	No	110	SAT	SAT	SAT
Wright	1969	47	8	Conduct Problems	No	No	12	ITBS	ITBS	—
Zbinden	1970	74	8–12	EMR	No	No	48	—	MAT	—

LEGEND:

MAT – Metropolitan Achievement Tests
IRI – Informal Reading Inventory
SRA – Selected Reading Activities
SAT – Stanford Achievement Tests
DRS – Durrell Reading Scales
WRAT – Wide Range Achievement Test
CAT – California Achievement Test
NYAT – New York Achievement Test

IST – Individual Spelling Tests
GATES – Gates—MacGinitie or McKillop or Oral Reading
Gil. – Gilmore Oral Reading Test
ITBS – Iowa Test of Basic Skills
GRAY – Gray Oral Test

Table 5

Median Coefficients Associated with
ITPA Subtests and Measures of Academic Performance

(Decimals Omitted)

	ITPA Subtests												
Academic Abilities	AR	VR	AA	VA	VE	ME	GC	ASM	VSM	VC	AC	SB	Composite
Reading	24	25	*39*	27	21	NS	*42*	31	24	NS	29	*38*	*42*
Spelling	NS	NS	NS	NS	NS	NS	*41*	NS	NS	NS	NS	31	30
Arith-metic	31	24	*40*	31	25	22	*40*	27	26	NS	NS	NS	*51*

Note: NS = Not statistically significant at the .05 level of confidence.

have little practical value. The predictive relationship between the subtests and reading is reduced further when median coefficients drawn from the five studies that provided control for intelligence are examined. Under this condition, only the Grammatic Closure subtest maintains a practically significant correlation ($r = .38$). This suggests that the relationship of Auditory Association, Sound Blending, and the Composite Score with reading may reflect the mutual intercorrelations of these variables with mental ability.

The ITPA and Spelling. The relationship of the ITPA subtests to spelling has been explored in fewer studies and 178 relevant correlation coefficients have been reported. The median correlation coefficients reported in table 5 reveal that only Grammatic Closure related to the criterion to a practically significant degree. Actually, Washington and Teska (1970) alone reported high positive correlations between most subtests and spelling skills. Zbinden (1970) found that only Grammatic Closure was highly related to four types of spelling tasks, while other authors reported either negligible or nonsignificant relationships for all subtests and spelling activities. Among the latter is the work of Hammill, Parker, and Newcomer (1975), the only study in which the effects of mental ability were controlled. Although it seems relatively certain that most ITPA subtests are not useful predictors of spelling skill, further studies which control for mental ability would provide useful information regarding the value of the Grammatic Closure subtest.

The ITPA and Arithmetic. In the literature reviewed, a total of 154 coefficients between the ITPA subtests and measures of arithmetic were reported. Results were quite similar to those reported in the reading section, as only Grammatic Closure, Auditory Association, and the Composite Score demonstrated practically significant predictive coefficients. Once again, however, in the study which controlled for mental age, none of the subtests reached the .35 level established for practical usefulness (Hammill et al., 1975). In any event, only two of the twelve ITPA subtests have any support for being useful predictors of arithmetic, and even those two could be questioned on the grounds that the influence of intelligence has not been adequately controlled for in most of the studies reviewed.

In conclusion, several important points emerge from the review of the concurrent correlation research. Most significant is the indication that nine of the twelve ITPA subtests lack predictive validity for any aspect of academic achievement studied. At best, only Auditory Association, Grammatic Closure, Sound Blending, and the Composite Score evidenced any predictive validity; however, when the influence of intelligence is controlled for, the coefficients associated with Auditory Association, Sound Blending, and the Composite Score drop below the established level for practical significance.

Although Grammatic Closure is the only subtest to remain significantly and practically correlated with academic achievement when mental ability is controlled, conclusions about the "true" extent of this relationship must be made with caution. Grammatic Closure is a test of standard English morphology, i.e., the use of linguistic inflections or markers such as plurals or possessives. Linguistic measures of this type are highly influenced by sociological factors such as race and social class, variables which have extensive influence on school performance. Until the effects of these factors on the relationship between Grammatic Closure and academic achievement are known for sure, one should be cautious in making statements about the value of this subtest. Hopefully, conclusive research is forthcoming.

Longitudinal Correlation Research

We found only four studies (Mueller, 1969; Hirshoren, 1969; Westinghouse Learning Corporation, 1969; Egeland et al., 1970) in which the usefulness of the ITPA subtests as long-term predictors of academic performance was investigated. In each of these, a group of children was administered the ITPA; then after a time interval exceeding nine months, they were administered various standardized tests of academic achievement; and the two sets of data were correlated.

The conclusions of these studies are in agreement in reporting that only Auditory Association is a practically useful predictor of *reading* and that Auditory Reception, Visual Reception, Verbal Expression, and Manual Expression are not useful predictors of any academic variables. The findings pertaining to the other subtests yielded very mixed results. Hirshoren reported that five of the subtests were good predictors of *spelling*, but his conclusions were contradicted by those of the Westinghouse study. Review of the coefficients depicting the relationship between the ITPA subtests and measures of *arithmetic* are most perplexing. For example, Hirshoren's work provides solid support for the ability of all of the ITPA subtests to predict arithmetic over time; the Westinghouse study, however, provides only a mosaic pattern of support; and Mueller reported that none of the coefficients associated with the subtests were statistically significant in his study. As none of these studies adequately controlled for mental ability, social class, or chronological age, one might argue that all of these coefficients are actually likely to be overestimations of the actual relationships. This being the case, it would be hazardous to assert that any of the ITPA subtests have been demonstrated to be good long-term predictors of academic success.

The confusion relating to the longitudinal results may be due to the fact that:

1. too few studies were available to analyze which made it difficult for trends to emerge,
2. the studies employed different tests of academic achievement,
3. the investigations used subjects of varying ages and types,
4. the time interval between testings differed drastically among the studies, and
5. the subjects were exposed to quite divergent instructional programs during the interval between test administrations.

It is particularly unfortunate that we could locate no studies which evaluated the psycholinguistic competencies of preschool-aged children and followed them up through the second or third grade. Studies such as these would be particularly decisive in demonstrating that psycholinguistic deficits diagnosed in young children are related developmentally to the academic difficulties so commonly observed in children during the later school years. Until this type of research has been done *and replicated*, one must conclude that the pertinent investigations which are currently available have failed to establish conclusively that the ITPA is a useful long-term predictor for reading, spelling, or arithmetic.

Review of Diagnostic Validity Research

The educational diagnostic validity of the ITPA subtests can be established by demonstrating that they discriminate significantly among groups of children who differ in academic competence. In fact, this approach has been used rather extensively in studies probing the relationship of the ITPA to reading. Regrettably, too few authors have investigated the areas of arithmetic or spelling to warrant review in this chapter. The researchers who are included in this chapter selected two or three groups of children on the basis of their reading proficiency. The mean (average) scores for each group on each of the twelve ITPA subtests were determined and compared to see if they differed significantly, usually using a *t*-test or an analysis of variance technique.

In all but five instances the studies reviewed used typical, elementary-school-aged children as subjects; the exceptions involved educable retarded and "learning disabled" youngsters. The cumulative results of these investigations are presented in table 6. A "+" is used when the author reported that a subtest significantly discriminated among the reading groups. An "0" signifies that the subtest failed to differentiate. Blank spaces occur in the table because some authors used the nine subtest experimental version of the ITPA (1961), others used the twelve subtest edition (1968), and still others used only selected subtests. In our review, no distinction is made between the editions, and the terminology of the 1968 version is used. Seemingly the changes made in the test revision were minor, and the basic constructs presented in the initial version were maintained in the later edition.

The percentage of analyses which reported subtest success in discriminating among divergent groups of readers is presented in table 7. So that the influence of mental ability might be clearly perceived, analyses from ten studies which covaried the effects of intelligence are separated from those obtained from ten studies which did not. Successful discrimination in 50 percent of the analyses was arbitrarily

Table 6

Results of Studies which Investigated
the Diagnostic Value of the ITPA for Reading

	IQ CONTROL	AR	VR	AA	VA	VE	ME	GC	ASM	VSM	VC	AC	SB
Bartin (1971)	YES	0	0	0	0	0	0	0	0	0	0	+	+
Bruininks et al. (1970)	NO	+	0	+	0	0	0	+	+	0	0	0	
Bruininks et al. (1970)	NO	0	0	+	0	0	0	0	0	0	0	0	
Deese (1971)	NO	+	0	0	+	0	+	0	+	+	0	0	+
Elkins (1972)	YES	0	0	0	0	0	0	0	0	0	0	0	+
Elkins (1972)	NO	+	0	0	+	0	+	0	+	0	0	+	0
Estes (1970)	NO			+	0	+	0	+	+	0	0	0	+
Golden & Steiner (1969)	YES			0	0	0	0	0	0	0	0		
Goodstein et al.* (1970)	YES	0	0	0	+	0	0	0	0	0,+			
Graubard (1965)	NO	0	0	0	+	0	0	+	0	+			
Hammill et al. (1975)	YES	0	0	0	0	0	0	0	0	0	0	0	0
Hammill et al. (1974)	YES		0	0	0	0	0	0	0				
Hepburn (1968)	YES	0	0	+	0	0	+	0	+	+	0	0	
Hyatt (1968)	NO	+	0	0	+	+	0	+	0	0			
Ikeda (1971)	NO	0	0	+	+	0	0	0	0	+	0	0	0
Kass (1966)	NO	0	+	+	0	0	0	0	0	0			
Kier (1963)	NO	0	0	0	0	0	0	0	0	+			
Larsen et al. (1974)	NO	0	0	0	0	0	0	+	+	0			0
Macioni (1969)	NO	+	0	+	0	0	+	+	+	0	+	0	0
Merlin (1971)	YES	0	0	0	0	0	0	+	+	+	+	0	
Ragland (1964)	NO	+	0	0	0	0	0	0	0	0			
Ruhly (1971)	YES	0	0	+	0	0	0	0	0	0	0	0	0
Sears (1969)	NO	0	0	0	0	0	0	0	0	0	0	0	0
Sumner (1966)	YES	+	0	0	0	0	0	0	0	0			

*Goodstein et al. correlated a battery of tests which included the ITPA subtests with a measure of reading, took the best five predictors, and included them in a discriminate analysis of two groups of good and poor readers. Only the VSM subtest correlated highly enough with reading($r = .40$) to be included in the discriminate portion of his study. Consequently, "0s" are recorded for all other subtests in this table. They reported that VSM discriminated between groups when the subjects had "low IQs" but did not when they had average IQs.

Table 7

*Percentage of Significant Discriminations
among Divergent Reading Groups by
ITPA Subtests with and without Control for IQ*

(Decimals Omitted)

	AR	VR	AA	VA	VE	ME	GC	ASM	VSM	VC	AC	SB
					ITPA SUBTEST							
Without IQ Control	31	08	46	31	15	15	52	43	36	17	17	57
With IQ Control	25	00	22	11	00	13	25	20	20	17	17	33
Total	29	05	36	23	10	24	43	33	28	17	17	46

selected as the minimal level necessary to establish diagnostic validity for reading.

Inspection of table 7 indicates that the consensus of all the investigations into the ITPA's diagnostic validity is that none of the subtests discriminate among reading groups. In studies which did not control for mental ability some support is found for the validity of the Grammatic Closure and Sound Blending subtests, while investigators who did covary the effects of IQ found no support for these subtests. Therefore, one may conclude that the existing research indicates that diagnosed psycholinguistic strengths and weaknesses based on the ITPA performance of school-aged children cannot be viewed as having any relationship to a child's observed difficulties in at least one basic school skill—reading.

Psycholinguistic Correlates
of Academic Achievement: A Study

In the earlier sections of this chapter we reviewed both the predictive and diagnostic validity research. The conclusions drawn from twenty-four correlational studies were that among the twelve ITPA subtests, only Grammatic Closure is a useful predictor of reading proficiency after intelligence has been controlled for. None of the subtests were related practically to arithmetic or spelling. Results of twenty studies dealing with the ITPA's diagnostic value were similarly discouraging since none of the subtests consistently differentiated between groups of proficient and deficient readers.

Although the results of these reviews appeared conclusive, one should not accept them too hastily for the following reasons: (1) only one of the studies performed both a correlative and a group-difference analysis using the same set of subjects; (2) few of the studies controlled for the influence of intelligence and several failed to control for the effects of age; (3) many authors used too few subjects, thus reducing the confidence one might have in their findings; and (4) while the relationship to reading was repeatedly investigated, the situation regarding arithmetic and spelling was relatively unexplored. Consequently, we along with Dr. R. Parker decided to design a study of the psycholinguistic-academic relationship which carefully avoided these difficulties.

Study Procedures

The subjects were 137 children who were similar to those used in the standardization sample for the 1968 revision of the ITPA. The children belong to the middle-socioeconomic class, and did not display behaviors suggestive of sensory, perceptual-motor, or social-emotional disturbance. They were selected from twelve fourth grade classes in five schools located in Chester County, Pennsylvania, and ranged in age from 105 to 118 months (mean age: 112 months). The California Short Form Intelligence Test was used to measure the children's general mental ability; the IQ's ranged from 87 to 111 (the mean was 97).

A short-form version of the ITPA was constructed for use in this study. The reliability and validity of this measure was demonstrated to be acceptable (Newcomer, 1973; Newcomer et al., 1974), which ensured the applicability of the ITPA with children of this age. This procedure is especially necessary when the test is used with older children because of potential ceiling effects which can cause truncated correlations. Academic achievement was measured by the California Achievement Test (CAT) which yielded information concerning reading, spelling, and arithmetic. The ITPA and CAT were administered in April, May, September, and October, 1972.

Two kinds of data analysis were deemed necessary to fully explore the relationships among the variables of interest in this study. First, a Pearson Product-Moment correlation matrix was computed with the effects of IQ partialled out using the formula suggested by Guilford (1956, p. 316). Second, the 137 subjects were divided into three groups, i.e., low, average, and high, based on their performance on each of the three academic variables studied, and thirty-six one-way analyses of covariance were run using IQ as the single covariate. A computer program of Scheffé's multiple comparison test was employed to test the differences among means for the trichotomized groups (Parker, 1971).

Results and Discussion

Predictive Relationships. A correlation matrix comprised of coefficients depicting the relationships between the psycholinguistic and the achievement variables is presented in table 8. Because of the comparatively large number of subjects used in this study, coefficients of .17 or greater are statistically significant at beyond the .05 level of confidence. Of the thirty-six coefficients in the matrix, twenty-seven are significant.

Using .35 as the cutoff point between coefficients with practical usefulness and those without, only five of the thirty–six coefficients evidence predictive validity. Of the twelve ITPA subtests, Auditory

Table 8

*Correlation Coefficients Depicting
the Relationship between the ITPA Subtests and
Three Measures of Academic Achievement*

*(Coefficients with IQ Partialled
Out Appear in Parentheses)* [1]

Psycholinguistic Abilities	Academic Abilities		
	Reading	*Spelling*	*Arithmetic*
Aud. Rec.	34 (16)	23 (05)	33 (16)
Vis. Rec.	32 (06)	15 (-11)	32 (10)
Verb. Exp.	28 (09)	23 (07)	24 (07)
Man. Exp.	18 (12)	16 (10)	21 (16)
Aud. Seq. Mem.	29 (21)	07 (-06)	22 (13)
Vis. Seq. Mem.	09 (-02)	12 (03)	08 (-03)
Aud. Assoc.	45 (22)	34 (12)	43 (22)
Vis. Assoc.	25 (06)	27 (13)	23 (06)
Gram. Clos.	57 (38)	38 (15)	51 (31)
Vis. Clos.	34 (18)	16 (-02)	32 (16)
Aud. Clos.	22 (11)	03 (-11)	05 (-10)
Sd. Blend.	29 (10)	18 (00)	24 (06)

[1]All data are two place decimals.
  N = 137
  df = 135
  P_{os} = .17

Association and Grammatic Closure alone seem to consistently and adequately predict academic achievement variables. However, when the influence of IQ is controlled for, only one coefficient, i.e., that associated with Grammatic Closure and Reading (.38), can be considered to be of practical value in prediction.

Diagnostic Relationships. In light of the findings which dealt with correlational relationships, it is not surprising to learn that after controlling for IQ few of the ITPA subtests discriminated among the groups of children who differed in three types of academic performance. Of the ITPA subtests, only Grammatic Closure and Auditory Association demonstrated any diagnostic validity. Of all the subtests, Grammatic Closure evidenced the most significant discriminating power, distinguishing among the achievement groups on both reading and arithmetic; Auditory Association discriminated only on the arithmetic variable. Neither of these subtests discriminated among the low-middle-high groups on spelling. The remaining ten subtests did not discriminate among the groups on any of the three academic measures. Of the thirty–six covariance analyses only three were statistically significant at the .05 level of confidence and two of these could be chance findings (36 analyses times .05 level of confidence equals two possible chance values). The adjusted means and associated *F* ratios are presented in table 9. Application of Scheffe's procedure for multiple comparisons to the three significant analyses revealed that all the other multiple comparisons were significant.

Only Grammatic Closure, the most linguistic of the ITPA subtests, consistently related to academic achievement in that it evidenced both significant predictive and diagnostic validity in this study. Actually, two of the three significant findings reported in table 9 pertain to Grammatic Closure, and only Grammatic Closure correlated at a practically useful level with academic achievement after the effects of IQ were controlled for (table 8). This finding is compatible with the conclusions of other investigations which we reviewed previously. If there are chance findings in this study, they are likely to be associated with the Auditory Association subtest.

To conclude, the results of this investigation fail to support the hypothesis that psycholinguistic abilities tapped by the ITPA, except those which contribute to the Grammatic Closure subtest and possibly to the Auditory Association subtest, are related to academic proficiency. Therefore, the assumption that these particular abilities are essential to, or play a significant role in, attaining academic success seems questionable, at least, at the fourth grade level. The conclu-

Table 9

Adjusted Means and F Ratios on the
ITPA Subtests for Groups Trichotomized on Each of
Three Academic Ability Variables

Academic Abilities	$\bar{X}_L$	$\bar{X}_m$	$\bar{X}_H$	F
Reading:				
Aud. Rec.	20.97	21.77	21.73	2.2
Vis. Rec.	27.50	27.93	29.22	1.8
Verb. Exp.	11.93	12.27	13.41	1.3
Man. Exp.	11.38	11.93	11.97	0.7
Aud. Seq. Mem.	27.24	29.40	31.35	2.4
Vis. Seq. Mem.	20.06	20.84	20.25	0.5
Aud. Assoc.	14.82	15.48	15.84	1.7
Vis. Assoc.	13.52	13.94	13.84	0.5
Gram. Clos.	13.02	14.01	14.73	7.9†
Vis. Clos.	20.44	21.01	22.47	1.9
Aud. Clos.	10.58	11.06	10.92	0.8
Sd. Blend.	11.47	11.66	12.19	0.6
Spelling:				
Aud. Rec.	21.58	21.74	21.11	1.4
Vis. Rec.	28.31	28.84	27.53	1.8
Verb. Exp.	12.16	12.92	12.54	0.5
Man. Exp.	11.87	11.55	11.86	0.3
Aud. Seq. Mem.	30.77	28.52	28.65	1.2
Vis. Seq. Mem.	20.65	19.44	21.12	2.3
Aud. Assoc.	15.11	15.80	15.22	1.4
Vis. Assoc.	13.43	13.80	14.09	1.0
Gram. Clos.	13.54	14.16	14.08	1.6
Vis. Clos.	21.77	21.07	21.06	0.4
Aud. Clos.	11.17	10.66	10.72	1.1
Sd. Blend.	11.90	11.61	11.81	0.2
Arithmetic:				
Aud. Rec.	20.97	21.69	21.77	1.9
Vis. Rec.	27.98	28.49	28.23	0.3
Verb. Exp.	12.19	12.53	12.90	0.3
Man. Exp.	11.40	11.85	12.01	0.5
Aud. Seq. Mem.	28.47	28.73	30.89	1.1
Vis. Seq. Mem.	20.80	20.44	19.88	0.4
Aud. Assoc.	14.60	15.49	16.02	3.4*
Vis. Assoc.	13.43	14.01	13.81	0.9
Gram. Clos.	13.03	14.17	14.51	7.0†
Vis. Clos.	20.57	21.89	21.36	1.2
Aud. Clos	11.18	10.67	10.74	1.0
Sd. Blend.	11.59	11.73	12.01	0.2

*Significant at the .05 level.
†Significant at the .01 level.

sions emerging from this study assume added credence, however, in that they are consistent with those obtained in the vast majority of other studies which have investigated these particular issues.

Conclusions

In this chapter we have reviewed and analyzed the results of forty different studies which were concerned with the predictive and diagnostic validity of the ITPA, and we have presented a replication study which dealt with both of these dimensions. The overall conclusions of our review are summarized in table 10. The contents of the table are arranged so that the consensus findings can be compared readily with those which resulted from the replication study. A "Yes" entry implies that the validity of the subtest was supported; a blank entry indicates the contrary; and a "Maybe" entry means that validity is supported if one disregards the influence of intelligence on the relationship.

If one maintains that only the results from which the influence of mental ability have been extracted can be considered with confidence, then Grammatic Closure alone among the subtests would have demonstrated validity. Both predictive and diagnostic validity of this subtest for reading is strongly indicated, and there is some evidence that it has diagnostic validity for arithmetic as well. One would have to conclude, however, that reading, arithmetic, and spelling were quite unrelated to the other skills measured by the ITPA.

On the other hand, if we accept the "Maybe" designations as indicative of support for validity, one could then point out that Grammatic Closure evidenced both predictive and diagnostic value for all academic abilities, that Auditory Association has some support for reading and arithmetic, and that Sound Blending might possibly be useful in the area of reading. Even applying this less stringent criterion, one finds that nine of the twelve subtests have no relationship with any area of academic achievement.

It is interesting to note the striking similarity between the results of the cumulative findings and those reported in our replication research. The only discrepancies were that our investigation showed Sound Blending to be less valid and Auditory Association to be more valid than did the consensus findings.

As only four longitudinal studies were found, they were too few to include in our table. The only consistent result which emerged from that research was that the Auditory Association subtest appears to predict reading.

Table 10

Summarization of Research Findings Relating to
Predictive and Diagnostic Validity of the ITPA Subtests

| | CONSENSUS | | | | Our Replication Study | | | | | |
| | Predictive Validity | | | Diagnostic Validity | Predictive Validity | | | Diagnostic Validity | | |
	Reading	Spelling	Arithmetic	Reading	Reading	Spelling	Arithmetic	Reading	Spelling	Arithmetic
AR										
VR										
AA	MAYBE		MAYBE		MAYBE		MAYBE			YES
VA										
VE										
ME										
GC	YES	MAYBE	MAYBE	MAYBE	YES	MAYBE	MAYBE	YES		YES
ASM										
VSM										
VC										
AC										
SB	MAYBE			MAYBE						

The consensus of this research permits us to make several summary statements concerning certain assumptions and practices involving the use of the ITPA in the schools. In addition, we will offer several suggestions for further study.

The fundamental premise underlying the widespread use of the ITPA in the schools is that the test has practical educational value, i.e., that it can be used to identify deficits which underlie academic failure. The existing research literature fails to validate this assumption. This being the case, the ITPA cannot be used with confidence to identify those young school-aged children who are likely to develop academic problems later in school. Neither can it be used with older children to diagnose specific psycholinguistic deficits which are causing their problems with reading, arithmetic, or spelling. In other words, for school-aged children, the existence of any specific psycholinguistic difficulties as determined by the ITPA has not been proved to be related to the achievement problems which they may currently exhibit or which they may develop in the future.

These statements apply not only to individuals who would utilize specific ITPA subtests to develop educational programs for children but also to those who would use test profiles as the basis for making general conclusions about children's particular "learning styles," i.e., the manner in which they use their sensory modalities, conceptual levels, and receptive, organizing, and expressive abilities to process information.

Instructional programming based on individual and/or group characteristics pertaining to sensory channel preferences (modality) is particularly common in education. For example, Kirk and McCarthy (1969) report that children who evidence superiority in certain visual processing skills probably require programmed instruction in reading which involves the use of a "look-and-say" approach, while children with basic deficits on visual subtests would require phonic training.

Our results would suggest that while certain groups of individuals may produce characteristic patterns of modality strengths and weaknesses, this information has no empirically demonstrated relevance for academic instruction. Since none of the visual and few of the auditory subtests relate significantly to reading, spelling, or arithmetic, it would be erroneous to conclude that the apparent superior performance on the visual subtests made by any individual or group of children means that they will learn academic skills better if materials are presented through visual means. A similar statement could be made regarding the auditory-vocal subtests.

Our data negates the value of references to children's conceptual levels (i.e., representational, automatic) as being significant for instruction. Since the educational relevance of most of the ITPA sub-tests was not demonstrated, it can be assumed that the concept of conceptual level is irrelevant as well. In other words, diagnosticians who would design remedial educational programs that incorporate a child's strengths and weaknesses in either automatic or representational level skills are proceeding without empirical justification. For example, when encountering a child who has both a reading problem and automatic level deficits, it is unwarranted to assume that the two are related. A remedial program designed to enhance automatic skills should not be prescribed in the hope that improvements will generalize to reading.

Finally, there is no support for generalizations which intimate that academic improvements may be gained by programming for children on the basis of their particular deficits in psycholinguistic processes (i.e., reception, organizing, and expression). Subtests measuring the receptive and expressive skills were found to be totally unrelated to academic achievement. Although the Auditory Association subtest may be related to reading and arithmetic, the Visual Association subtest is not; therefore, one cannot conclude that associative processes per se relate to achievement. In short, the usefulness of the process construct for educational purposes is far from established.

In our opinion, the results of this research have extremely important implications for school practice. There appears little doubt that, when used with school-aged children, the ITPA's value is limited to gathering broad, descriptive information regarding certain of their learning characteristics; its use for individual diagnosis is neither supported nor recommended. Specifically, the test should not be used for the purposes of (1) determining the cause of academic failure, (2) devising strategies for the remediation of academic problems, (3) selecting instructional programs designed to match a child's psycholinguistic characteristics, and (4) screening individual children to locate those who have a high probability of failing basic school subjects.

Let us be the first to point out that these findings deal with the ITPA as it relates to academic learning. The conclusions regarding its lack of practical value should not be generalized to the area for which it was developed—psycholinguistics. It is conceivable that if the test were applied exclusively in the area of psycholinguistics and not used in relationship to reading, spelling, or arithmetic its value might be established. For a discussion of the test's validity in areas other than academics, the reader is referred to the section on validity in chapter 2.

Our review of the research that is concerned with the ITPA's educational utility revealed areas which require further investigation. For example:

1. The long-term predictive value of the ITPA has never been investigated adequately. A study should be designed in which the test is administered to a large sample of children aged three or four. Their linguistic and academic growth could then be monitored consistently as they progressed through the school years. This would answer once and for all the very important question: Do very young children who evidence various psycholinguistic weakness have a higher incidence of academic problems later in life than similar young children who are psycholinguistically intact? If so, what kinds of school-related problems do they develop?

2. A concentrated study should be made of the Grammatic Closure subtest's relationship to academic achievement in order to determine for sure that the correlation is actually predicated on the association of morphological competence to academic achievement rather than on the association of age, social class, or racial background to academic achievement.

3. All validity studies should be replicated using children who have severe psycholinguistic handicaps. Additional studies in this area which use normal, retarded, or academically lagging elementary aged children are probably not warranted.

4. Diagnostic validity studies should be undertaken which group subjects according to their psycholinguistic abilities and test them on reading, spelling, and arithmetic to determine the extent to which academic abilities discriminate among the ITPA defined groups.

4

Effectiveness of Psycholinguistic Training

Introduction

The original Osgood schema and the Kirk adaptation of that model have provided the incentive for the development of a multitude of instructional procedures which have been published in recent years. These procedures, which include teaching manuals, methods books, and systematic training programs, are intended to stimulate the general psycholinguistic development of those children who are apparently "lagging" behind their peers or to remediate specific abilities in children who evidence identifiable deficits. Although they vary markedly in format, comprehensiveness, and procedures governing use, these approaches display their indebtedness to the Osgood-Kirk principles by the constructs selected for training, the terminology used, and the definitions adhered to.

No effort will be made in this book to provide the reader with a detailed review of particular instructional programs. However, we will discuss briefly the kinds of programs which are available and provide ample references so that the interested reader might consult

This chapter is an expanded version of: D. Hammill and S. Larsen, "The Effectiveness of Psycholinguistic Training, *Exceptional Children* 41 (1974):5–15.

the original sources to gain full understanding of any particular approach. Our primary purpose in this chapter is to discuss the effectiveness of efforts to train psycholinguistic abilities in the schools. In order to do this, we will focus on the efficacy research.

Programs for Training
Psycholinguistic Abilities

Teachers or researchers who wish to implement psycholinguistic training in a school either design their own activities or use one of the several commercially available programs. In either case, once the program has been selected it is generally used in one of two ways. The goal of one approach is to improve the overall abilities of an entire group of children by exposing each child to approximately the same activities. These programs are often referred to as "developmental" training efforts. In the other approach, each child's specific psycholinguistic strengths and weaknesses are determined and a special instructional plan is prepared for him alone. These individualized programs, which emphasize the amelioration of any deficiencies that a child may have, are generally referred to as "remedial" training.

Two of the most popular developmental programs are those designed by Karnes (1968, 1972) and by Dunn and Smith (1966). These were developed originally for use with disadvantaged or retarded children rather than for use with remedial cases. This is indicated by the fact that their authors make little or no mention of differential diagnosis or of adapting the activities to fit individual pupil needs. On the other hand, the activities offered by Kirk and Kirk (1971), Minskoff, Wiseman, and Minskoff (1972), Farrald and Schamber (1973), and Bush and Giles (1969), among many others, are intended primarily for remedial use, though they can be adapted easily for developmental purposes as well. All of these authors stress the desirability of initial assessment (prior to training) and either provide the teacher with an evaluation device or give examples of appropriate assessment procedures. The activities which comprise several of the approaches, notably those of Minskoff, Wiseman, and Minskoff, Dunn and Smith, Karnes, and Bush and Giles, are carefully sequenced by age and with the exception of the Bush and Giles activities are accompanied by kits of supplemental materials, workbooks, etc. Those other approaches, advocated by Farrald and Schamber, Kirk and Kirk, and others, represent loose collections of unsequenced activities which are apparently intended to serve as examples of appropriate techniques rather than as comprehensive programs.

The manner in which many of the training programs incorporate the ITPA constructs can be demonstrated clearly by examination of the MWM Program for Developing Language Activities (Minskoff, Wiseman, and Minskoff, 1972). The program is designed to remediate disabilities in all areas represented by the ITPA. Materials include a screening inventory which is used by teachers to rate children in eleven of twelve areas measured by the ITPA subtests. (Auditory Closure and Sound Blending are combined into a single section.) Instructional methods are organized into six manuals: Auditory and Visual *Reception*, Auditory and Visual *Association*, Manual and Verbal *Expression*, Auditory and Visual *Memory*, Grammatic and Visual *Closure*, and *Auditory Closure—Sound Blending*. Each of these manuals contains a series of activities which may be used to increase a child's competence in particular psycholinguistic areas. Specific examples of the kinds of instructional tasks subsumed under each of the areas follow.

Psycholinguistic Areas	*Instructional Tasks*
Auditory Reception	Orally present the noun "car" in conjunction with pictures of cars.
Visual Reception	Make oral and graphic presentations of color concepts such as the word "red" in association with a tangible object such as a red block.
Auditory Association	Teach recognition of category member by asking questions such as "Is a girl a person or a toy?"
Visual Association	Have the child complete number sequences presented graphically and orally. Example "What number should come next, 4, 2, 4, 2, 4, __ ?"
Verbal Expression	Assign a descriptive word to an expression. For example, the child looks at a smiling face and repeats the word "happy."
Manual Expression	Have the child trace a raised surface such as a sandpaper letter.
Auditory Memory	Have a child follow a set of oral directions such as "Stand up or Sit down."

Visual Memory	Have a child memorize a sequence of shapes such as circle and triangle and then identify which has been removed.
Auditory Closure	Ask the child to repeat a sentence spoken against a background of interfering sounds.
Grammatic Closure	Have the child imitate spoken sentences.
Visual Closure	Have the child find partially hidden objects.
Sound Blending	Present syllables of words such as "ba-by" and have the child blend the syllables into a whole word.

Assumptions Which Underlie Training

Most of those individuals who advocate these programs accept certain key premises as true. In the first place, they assume that discrete elements of language behavior are identifiable and measurable. They believe that diagnostic procedures which incorporate the findings derived from various supplemental language tests with those from clinical experience can be used to accurately delimit a child's specific language needs. Second, they assume that these particular psycholinguistic skills provide the underpinnings for much school-related learning. In other words, a child who cannot demonstrate adequate competency in these abilities can be expected to fail in school activities such as reading, writing, arithmetic, and spelling. Third, they accept as valid the hypothesis that defective psycholinguistic skills can to some extent be improved through training. Fourth, they believe that these increased abilities will generalize to improve classroom learning.

Information which relates to the first assumption was covered in chapter 2, at least with regard to the ITPA. The second and fourth assumptions were dealt with and refuted in chapter 3. The validity of the third assumption is the province of this chapter. In this part of the book, we will focus on the effects of psycholinguistic training on the improvement of psycholinguistic skills. Certainly there is every reason to conclude that gains caused by such training efforts should be most apparent in language related skills. Practically all of the efficacy research which we have reviewed relates to this topic. Unfortunately, the effects of such training on academic abilities is relatively unexplored at the present time.

Characteristics of Training Studies

Only studies which used the ITPA or one or more of its subtests as the criterion for improvement of language behavior were reviewed for this chapter. Since the ITPA is based primarily upon the constructs of Osgood (1957) and since most of the training programs were generated either from the ITPA or from the original Osgood theory, it was felt that this stipulation would be the most efficient in determining the effectiveness of psycholinguistic training. It was also assumed that the researchers who conducted these studies believed that there was some relationship between the ITPA and their intervention programs or they would not have selected this test to demonstrate the effects of their program.

The characteristics of the studies reviewed are presented in table 11. The table includes:

1. the names of the researchers;
2. the publication date of the research;
3. the number of subjects;
4. the type of subjects;
5. the age of the experimental group;
6. the approach to training, e.g., prescriptive (individualized) where a special program is designed for a child on the basis of diagnostic procedures or general (nonindividualized) where children are exposed to an overall language stimulation program;
7. the specific kind of experimental training, e.g., selected activities based on an ITPA-psycholinguistic model (usually author-designed but similar to the Kirk and Kirk (1971) or Bush and Giles (1969) activities), the Peabody Language Development Kits (PLDK), or other teaching systems;
8. the estimated duration of the treatment period; and
9. the number of hours devoted to training.

The following example demonstrates how the table should be read. In 1967, Mueller and Dunn evaluated the effectiveness of the PLDK, a general, nonindividualized approach to teaching language. Their experimental and control subjects were elementary-school-aged, educable mentally retarded children. More than twenty subjects were in each group. The experimental subjects received in excess of fifty hours of training over a more than twenty week period.

Table 11
Characteristics of Psycholinguistic Training Studies

Authors	Date	E Ss	C Ss	TYPE	AGE	APPROACH	EXP. METHOD	EHT	DOT
Blessing	1964	2	2	1	UTE	2	1	3	2
Blue	1970	2	2	2	UTE	2	1	1	2
Bradley et al.	1966	2	2	2	2+3	1	1	3	3
Carter	1966	3	3	3	2	2	2	2	3
Clasen et al.	1969	2	2	3	2	2	2	3	1
Crutchfield	1964	1	1	1+2	2+3	2	2	1	2
Dickie	1968	3	3	3	1	2	3	1	3
Dunn & Mueller	1966	3	3	3	2	2	2	3	3
Dunn & Mueller	1967	3	3	3	2	2	2	3	3
Ensminger	1966	3	3	3	2	2	2	3	3
Forgnone	1967	3	3	1	2	2	2	2	2
Gazdic	1971	3	2	4	2	2	2	3	3
Gibson	1966	2	2	1	2	2	3	2	3
Gray & Klaus	1965	3	3	3	1	2	3	3	3
Guess et al.	1969	3	3	2	3	2	2	3	3
Hart	1963	1	1	4	2	1	1	3	1
Hartman	1967	3	3	3	1	1	1	3	3
Hodges & Spicker	1967	2	2	3	1	2	3	UTE	3
Jones	1970	3	3	3	1	2	2	2	2
Karnes et al.	1970	3	3	3	1	2	1	3	3
Lavin	1971	3	3	3	1	2	3	3	3
Leiss	1974	3	3	2	2+3	2	1	3	3
McConnell et al.	1969	3	3	3	1	2	3	3	3
Minskoff	1967	1	1	1	3	1	1	1	1
Mitchell	1968	3	3	3	1	2	2	UTE	3
Morgan	1972	3	3	3	1	2	3	3	3
Morris	1967	*	*	*	*	2	2	3	3
Mueller & Dunn	1967	3	3	1	2	2	2	3	3
Painter	1966	1	1	3	1	2	3	3	1
Runyon	1970	2	2	1	2	2	1	2	3
Saudargas et al.	1970	2	1	1	2	1	2	1	2

Author	Year	Subject Numbers	Type	Age	Approach	Exp. Method	Est. Hrs. of Training	Duration of Training
Sapir	1971	2	1	4	2	2	UTE	3
Schifani	1972	1	1	1	3	2	3	3
Siders	1970	3	3	3	2	2	1	3
Smith	1962	2	2	4	1	1	3	2
Spollen & Ballif	1971	3	3	3	1	1		3
Stearns	1967	2	1	3	1		2	2
Strickland	1967	3	3		2	2	UTE	2
Wiseman	1963	1	1	1	2	1	2	1

*Information not obtained

CODE:

Subject Numbers:
1 = 6 to 10
2 = 11 to 20
3 = 20+

Type
1 = EMR
2 = TMR
3 = Disadv.
4 = Other

Age
1 = preschool
2 = 6–11
3 = 11+

Approach
1 = Prescriptive/
     Individualized
2 = General/
     Nonindividualized

Exp. Method:
1. Selected activities. Based
    on ITPA Model
2. PLDK
3. Other

Est. Hrs. of Training
1 = 30
2 = 30–50
3 = 50+
UTE = Unable to Estimate

Duration of Training
1 = 10 weeks
2 = 10–20 weeks
3 = 20+ weeks

71

While some of the researchers compared the experimental subjects with a variety of contrast subjects, e.g., those who received remedial reading instruction or speech therapy, we were interested only in the experimental-control group analyses. In all instances, the results discussed in this review refer to comparisons between children trained in language and those who received no formal instruction of any kind or those who were enrolled in "traditional" programs.

Effects of Training Psycholinguistic Abilities

The findings of these studies are summarized in table 12. A "+" indicates that the author reported that the trained Ss (subjects) did considerably better than nontrained Ss on a particular ITPA subtest. An "0" indicates that the control Ss were equal to or better than the experimental Ss on a subtest analysis. In most of the cases "+" and "0" are the same as statistical significance (.05 level) or nonstatistical significance respectively. Where this is not the case, the author's name is numbered and a description of the procedures used to designate the study's analyses as "+" or "0" is presented in a footnote. The footnotes also explain those occasions where our interpretations of a study's findings differed from its author's.

The reader will notice the many blank spaces in table 12. This occurs because some authors used the nine subtest 1961 version of the ITPA and others used the twelve subtest 1968 version. Some researchers were concerned only with selected subtests, while others were interested in the ITPA total score and not at all in the subtests. The effects of training on Auditory Closure and Sound Blending are almost nonexistent which was probably due to the fact that these subtests only became available with the publication of the revised ITPA and are only supplemental tests in that version. Visual Closure is also a new subtest, but it is included in the ITPA proper and has, therefore, been studied more frequently.

For these analyses, no distinction is made between the 1961 and 1968 versions of the ITPA. To avoid confusion, the terminology of the more recent version is used throughout this review. It was our opinion that differences between the two tests were òf a technical nature, e.g., some subtests were lengthened, instructions were altered slightly, names of the subtests were changed, etc.; but the basic constructs of the two versions remained essentially the same. This opinion is supported by the recent work of Waugh (1973) who compared the tests and concluded that for most purposes they could be used interchangeably.

Table 12 should be read as follows: Sapir reported that special psycholinguistic instruction was beneficial in developing the abilities measured by Auditory Association, Verbal Expression, Manual Expression, Auditory Sequential Memory, and the total ITPA Language Age. Such training was found to be no more beneficial than that in traditional classes regarding Visual Reception, Visual Association, or Visual Sequential Memory. No analyses were undertaken pertaining to the remaining ITPA subtests.

The authors of the thirty-nine research studies* reported (or provided the necessary information which allowed us to calculate and report) the results of 280 comparisons between the performance of E and C *Ss* on the subtest scores and the total scores of the ITPA. Therefore, it was possible to compute the percentage of analyses which indicated that special psycholinguistic training was beneficial.

When integrating the information provided in tables 11 and 12, one can evaluate the effectiveness of such instruction on differing types of children, e.g., retarded, disadvantaged, preschool, elementary. The percentage of analyses, by subgroup, which found the intervention successful is found. in table 13. Where analyses were few, i.e., less than five, as was the case with Visual Closure, Auditory Closure, and Sound Blending, percentages were not computed.

Fifteen authors (103 analyses) studied the value of psycholinguistic training with retarded *Ss* with less than encouraging results. There was not a single subtest for which a majority of the researchers reported that training was beneficial. Therefore, the value of training retarded subjects in psycholinguistics has not been demonstrated to date.

The eighteen authors (154 analyses) who used the instruction with "disadvantaged" children were apparently more successful, especially regarding improvement in association and verbal expression skills. However, as the positive percentages are only in the 50s and as most of the subtests of the ITPA did not respond to instruction, support for training disadvantaged children in psycholinguistic skills is at best limited.

The effects of age on training was probed at the preschool level by fifteen authors (121 analyses) and at the elementary level by nineteen authors (143 analyses). Apparently the training programs used to

---

*The research of Sowell (1975) and of Pumfrey and Naylor (1975) became available after the tables were prepared for publication and therefore is not included in the analyses. Sowell investigated the effects of the Minskoff, Wiseman, Minskoff materials and concluded that their use did not stimulate either psycholinguistic or academic growth. Pumfrey and Naylor on the other hand were relatively successful using a combined PLDK and prescriptive approach.

Table 12

Results of Studies Which Attempted to
Train Psycholinguistic Processes

Researcher	ITPA SUBTESTS												
	AR	VR	AA	VA	VE	ME	GC	VC	ASM	VSM	AC	SB	Total
Blessing					+								
Blue													0
Bradley et al.[1]	+	+	0	+	+	+	+		0	0			+
Carter	+	+	+	+	+	+	+		+	+			+
Clasen et al.	0	+	0	+	0	0	0		0	0			0
Crutchfield[2]	+	0	0	0	0	0	0		0	+			0
Dickie			0		0								
Dunn & Mueller[3]	0	0	+	+	+	0	0		0	0			+
Ensminger	0	0	+	0	+	0	0		0	0			0
Forgnone													0
Gazdic													0
Gibson	0	0	0	0	0	0	0		0	0			0
Gray & Klaus	+	+	+	+	+	0	+		+	+			+
Guess et al.[4]													0
Hart[5]	0	0	+	+	+	+	0		+	+			+
Hartman	0	0	0	0	0	0	0		0	0			0
Hodges & Spicker													0
Jones[6]	+	0	0	0	+	+	0	0	0	0			0
Karnes et al.	0	+	+	0	0	0	+		0	0			+

See Footnotes. The number to the right of the name indicates the specific footnote.

1. Bradley et al. did not report the significance of difference in gain scores between E and C groups for the Auditory Sequential Memory subtest. Inspection of their Table 1 clearly indicates that the difference would be NS.

2. Crutchfield did no tests of significance but did provide pretest and posttest subtest means. It was therefore possible to calculate pre-post gains for E and C Ss. His E Ss were subdivided into a younger (n=9) and older (n=8) group, but no such division was made of the C Ss (n=15). Because of the similarity in the n's of the two E groups, they were combined and their mean gains compared with those of the C group. Of the nine subtests, the gains of five favored the C Ss; in two instances, the differences were two months or less; and only two cases, where the differences exceeded seven months, could be taken as positive evidence of training.

3. Dunn and Mueller undertook two studies, one dealt with the effects of training on the total ITPA score (1966), while the other dealt with the subtests (1967). No tests of significance were reported for the latter. Instead pretest and posttest means for the E and C groups and gain scores are provided. On four of the nine subtests, gains favored the C Ss and these are recorded as "0" in table 12. In addition two subtests, Auditory Reception and Visual Sequential Memory, are also recorded as "0." In each of these cases the difference between E and C groups on both the pretest and the posttest was less than two months. The result for Auditory Association, Visual Association, and Verbal Expression clearly demonstrated the positive effects of training and are recorded "+."

4. The Guess et al. sample was post tested twice—once at the end of the nine month training period and again nine months later. Differences between E and C groups were NS at the first testing but were significant at the last testing. The NS value is used in table 12 because "follow-up" research was not dealt with in this review.

5. Hart does no tests of significance of difference on his subtest data. He did provide the pretest and posttest means for his E and C groups. It was then possible to estimate gain scores. On one subtest, Auditory Reception, the gains favored the C group; on two others, Visual Reception and Grammatic Closure, the gains of the E

Table 12 (cont.)

Researcher	AR	VR	AA	VA	VE	ME	GC	VC	ASM	VSM	AC	SB	Total
						ITPA SUBTESTS							
Lavin	0	0	0	0	0	0	0	0	0	0			0
Leiss	0	0	0	0	0	0	0	0	0	0			0
McConnell et al.	+	0	+	+	+	+	+		+	+			+
Minskoff[7]				+	0	+			0	0			0
Mitchell	0	0	0	0	0	0	0		+	0			0
Morgan	0	0	+	+	+	0	0	+	0	0			+
Morris[8]			+		+		0						+
Mueller & Dunn	0		0				0			0			+
Painter	0	0	+	0	0	+	0		0	0			
Runyon													+
Saudargas et al.	0	0	0	0	0	0	0	0	0	0	0	0	+
Sapir		0	+	0	+	+			+	0			+
Schifani[9]	0	0	0	0	0	0	0	0	+	0			+
Siders	0		0		0		0						
Smith[10]	+	+	+	+	+	+	+		0	+			+
Spollen & Ballif													0
Stearns[11]	0	0	+	+	+	0	0		0	0			0
Strickland			+						+				0
Wiseman	0	0	0	0	+	+	0		+	0			+

group exceeded those of the C groups by four or fewer months. These subtests were arbitrarily recorded as "0." The other differences all favored the E group and ranged from five to twenty-four months.

6. Jones did no subtest analyses, though she did provide pre-post means for E and C groups (p. 119) which made it possible to compute gain scores for the groups. E gains were subtracted from C gains for each subtest and the total score. On an additional four subtests and the total score, the differences favored the E group by less than two points. These eight analyses are recorded as "0" in Table 12. The remaining three analyses favored the E group by differences ranging from 2.4 to 5.6 points and are recorded "+."

7. Minskoff uses the .10 level of confidence in his dissertation. As all other authors in this table employed the .05 level, we reinterpreted Minskoff's findings using the .05 level in order to be consistent.

8. Morris's work is a Master's degree thesis which we did not obtain. Our knowledge of its contents and conclusions is acquired from Dunn and Smith (1966).

9. In his dissertation, Schifani tests only the significance of the differences relating to the ITPA total score. As he provided means and standard deviations for the subtests, it was possible to compute the significance of subtest differences.

10. Smith reported no analyses regarding the significance of differences between E and C groups. It was possible, however, to compute the mean gain scores for the groups from data provided. The C Ss regressed or made no gain on five subtests and gains of less than three months on the four subtests, while the E Ss registered gains on all subtests ranging from three to thirteen months. In table 12, all the subtests with the exception of Auditory Sequential Memory are designated "+"; however, because of the small N, if analyses could have been run on these data, some of the results might have been NS.

11. Stearns only tested the significance of the differences between E and C groups on the total ITPA score. Subtest means were provided, but not the associated standard deviations. He concluded, from inspection, that training appeared to positively affect three of nine subtests.

date emphasize the development of auditory association abilities at the preschool level and expressive and general language abilities at the elementary level. Once again, the positive findings are limited to the representational level subtests and to the total ITPA score.

Eight of the researchers (70 analyses) used a prescriptive approach; i.e., they diagnosed their *Ss*, usually with the ITPA, and designed programs specifically for each child. This approach was apparently successful in stimulating visual associational and expressive language abilities. The nonindividualized approach to instruction, i.e., those approaches in which all children are exposed to a set program, was studied by thirty authors (208 analyses) and was evidently minimally effective in teaching auditory associational and verbal expressive abilities.

Two kinds of curricula were employed most often—the "selected activities" approach, used by thirteen researchers (85 analyses) and the PLDK approach, used by sixteen researchers (112 analyses). The selective activities approach was found to be useful in stimulating skills necessary to do well on the manual expressive subtest. With the exception of Verbal Expression, the PLDK does not seem to be an efficient method for developing language processes.

The figures at the bottom of table 13 denoted by "Total" are of particular interest in that they reflect the overall situation relative to psycholinguistic training accomplished to date. It is apparent that for the most part, researchers have been unsuccessful in developing those skills which would enable their subjects to do well on the ITPA. The Auditory Association and the Verbal Expression subtests seem to be the most responsive to intervention, while Visual Closure and Visual Sequential Memory are the most resistant.

Each ITPA subtest relates to a particular psycholinguistic construct in the Osgood-Kirk model, i.e., level, process, and channel (modality). By assigning each subtest to its appropriate construct and by computing the percentages of "+'s" it is possible to estimate the success which researchers have had in stimulating the theoretical psycholinguistic dimensions underlying the ITPA. These constructs, the subtests which comprise them, and the percentages of positive analyses are presented in table 14.

The collective results of the studies reviewed suggest that the idea that psycholinguistic constructs, as measured by the ITPA, can be trained by existing techniques remains nonvalidated. Comparatively speaking, the most encouraging findings pertained to training at the representational level, especially the expressive processes. The most discouraging results were associated with training at the automatic

Table 13

The Percentage of Analyses, by Subgroup,
Which Found Psycholinguistic Training to Be Successful

Subgroups	ITPA SUBTESTS												
	AR	VR	AA	VA	VE	ME	GC	VC	ASM	VSM	AC	SB	Total
Retarded Ss	33	25	13	33	40	44	22	—	22	20	—	—	50
Disadvantaged Ss	27	29	59	50	50	29	27	—	33	21	—	—	40
Preschool Ss	27	27	54	45	42	27	27	—	33	18	—	—	31
Elementary Ss	31	25	43	46	57	54	23	—	31	29	—	—	56
Prescriptive Approach	17	17	33	57	57	57	17	—	29	14	—	—	50
Nonindividualized Approach	32	28	52	39	50	33	25	20	37	26	—	—	46
Selected Activities	29	29	38	29	44	50	29	—	33	25	—	—	42
PLDK Activities	27	30	42	40	55	30	17	—	30	18	—	—	47
Total	**28**	**24**	**48**	**44**	**52**	**40**	**23**	**20**	**35**	**23**	**—**	**—**	**47**

Table 14

*Psycholinguistic Constructs, the ITPA
Subtests Which Comprise Them, and the
Percentage of Positive Analyses*

	Constructs	Subtests	Percentages
Levels	Representational	AR, VR, AA, VA, VE, ME	40
	Automatic	GC, VC, ASM, VSM, AC, SB	25
Processes	Reception	AR, VR	27
	Organization	AA, VA, GC, VC, ASM, VSM, AC, SB	33
	Expression	VE, ME	46
Modalities	Auditory-Vocal	AR, AA, VE, GC, ASM, AC, SB	37
	Visual-Motor	VR, VA, ME, VC, VSM	32

level, the receptive and organizing processes, and both the auditory-vocal and visual-motor modalities.

There is one additional observation worth noting—the more recent findings are considerably less encouraging regarding the benefits of training than are those of the earlier research. In the studies located, 110 experimental-control comparisons were made between 1962 and 1966; 73 comparisons were made between 1967 and 1969; and 98 between 1970 and 1973. The percentages supporting training were 52, 31, and 21 respectively. As we can generate no satisfactory explanation for this finding, we choose to merely report the observation without comment.

Additional analyses were undertaken to investigate the effects of hours of training and length of the training period on subject improvement. Since the results indicated these were not significant variables they are not reported.

Implications of the Findings
for School Practice

It seems as though we are confronted with four possible explanations which could account for the findings of this review:

1. The ITPA is an invalid measure of psycholinguistic functioning.
2. The intervention programs and/or techniques are inadequate.
3. Most psycholinguistic dimensions are either untrainable or highly resistant to stimulation.
4. There exists methodological inadequacies in the studies.

Influence of ITPA Validity on Training

One might argue that the ITPA is an inappropriate criterion to use as an indicator of a training program's success. If this were the case, then significant improvements in the psycholinguistic performance of children which were the results of training might go unrecorded due to the test's "low reliability" and "inadequate validity." There is some reason to suspect that this argument may have some merit, at least with regard to some of the ITPA subtests.

In table 2, chapter 2, the ITPA subtests are evaluated on four aspects of construct validity—independence, channel, process, and level purity. To any of these aspects the question can be asked, "Is a particular subtest valid?" and answered "Yes, possibly, or no." By assigning one point for each "yes" answer and one-half point for each "possibly" answer, one can convert each subtest's validity statement into quantitative form. Thus the "Validity Index" for Auditory Association is 4, that for Grammatic Closure is 2-½, and that for Visual Sequential Memory is 0.

This information was related to the percentages found in the row labeled "Total" in table 13 using Spearman's *Rho Rank Order* correlation procedure. The coefficient was computed using only nine ITPA subtests; Visual Closure, Auditory Closure, and Sound Blending were excluded because of their infrequent use in the training studies. The resultant coefficient is .85 which Guilford (1956) describes as a high correlation indicating a marked relationship. Consequently, the psycholinguistic abilities which were reported to respond the most favorably to training tended to be the same as those represented by valid ITPA subtests. In fact, four of the five most valid subtests are also the ones which profited the most from instruction.

The implication of this observation for training is most important. For example, if a researcher implements a program to develop psycholinguistic abilities and uses those ITPA subtests which are invalid to evaluate his subjects' progress, any change in them will likely go undetected. Therefore a distinct possibility exists that the rather disappointing results of the efficacy research concerning psycholinguistic training may be due in some degree to the selection of invalid ITPA subtests as criterion measures. This possibility, however, should not be used to "explain away" the overall negative conclusions regarding training which have accumulated in the research literature to date because the effects of training on the *valid* ITPA subtests have also been less than encouraging.

Since the use of certain ITPA subtests as criterion measures is questionable, researchers who would demonstrate the effectiveness of particular psycholinguistic training programs might want to consider other alternatives. For example, perhaps they should carefully analyze the contents of their particular intervention programs and develop criterion-referenced measures to correspond with the specific skills being taught. In this way the measures used to evaluate a pupil's improvement would bear a marked relationship to the curricula.

Adequacy of the Training Programs

It seems likely that the instructional programs are uneven in that they seem to emphasize training associative and expressive abilities to the comparative exclusion of training receptive and automatic skills. This may be inherent in the programs, or teachers may avoid such activities and show preference for the associative and expressive activities. In any event, various psycholinguistic abilities are apparently not being taught using the presently available instructional systems.

Trainability of Psycholinguistic Processes

The positive findings regarding Verbal Expression suggest that at least one of the skills tapped by the ITPA may be responsive to training. This leads one to speculate that under different situations using improved techniques, others might also respond to instruction. Still, the results of the review strongly indicate that neither the ITPA subtests nor their theoretical constructs are equally ameliorable. Approximately 70 percent or better of the analyses were unsuccessful in training Grammatic Closure, Visual Sequential Memory, Visual Closure, Auditory or Visual Reception, automatic level skills, receptive processes, or visual-motor modality skills.

Methodological Inadequacies

Knowledge that the available research findings have been for the most part unsupportive of psycholinguistic training has prompted some educators to question the appropriateness of using traditional pretest–posttest experimental-control group designs. They point out with some justification that there might exist within any group of children who have both academic and psycholinguistic problems a subgroup for whom the training was beneficial and that the significant progress of this subgroup of children was lost when their scores were combined with those of other children. To retrieve this information, they recommend that "N-of-one" studies be substituted, at least in part, for traditional designs.

The case history approach, i.e., the N-of-one study, is a time-honored procedure in psychology, education, and all clinical fields of study. It provides for the in depth, analytic observation of a single child and no technique is really its equal for generating hypotheses or for determining the sequences of linguistic (C. Chomsky, 1969) or cognitive (Piaget, 1955) development. Yet, the procedure has serious limitations when used to test the efficacy of a training program, especially when the attempt is being made to train skills which are closely related to age. To use the N-of-one study in this manner is the equivalent of implementing a pretest–posttest intervention study with a single subject and no control group. Since all of the psycholinguistic abilities measured by the ITPA improve to some extent as a function of the child's growing older, all N-of-one studies should report significant gains eventually. Such an approach may have value in aiding professionals to understand more fully psycholinguistic development in children, but we fear it cannot realistically be employed to demonstrate the effectiveness of this or that remedial program or activity.

If needed there were a subgroup of children for whom a systematic, structured psycholinguistic program might be beneficial, it would most certainly have specific characteristics which could be used to identify suitable subjects for study. Research could then be designed to demonstrate that, on this sample at least, training would result in substantial improvements.

One of the major implications to be drawn from this review of research is that the efficacy of training psycholinguistic functionings has not been conclusively demonstrated. Whether some of the subtests are unresponsive to instructional efforts because they are basically impossible or extremely difficult to teach, because the training programs do not provide sufficient attention to them, because the ITPA subtests are not appropriate measures of these constructs, or because of the use of inadequate research methodology, we cannot say. This is a matter for future research to clarify.

These findings are of importance when considering the amount of time, effort, and money that is currently being devoted to providing children with training designed to increase psycholinguistic skills. A concerted effort should now be made by the advocates of such training to determine conclusively that the constructs are in fact trainable by available programs and/or to identify the characteristics of the children for whom this type of training is beneficial. Until these results are available, however, programs designed to improve psycholinguistic functioning need to be viewed cautiously and monitored with care so that children experiencing difficulty in school will not be subjected to irrelevant activities that will only result in a waste of valuable time.

5

Psycholinguistic Training Today: A View from Its Advocates

For the most part, the preceding four chapters of this book have presented what we feel is a thorough analysis of the ITPA constructs, including their relationship to current psycholinguistic theory and their functional value for educational application. The conclusions, which were based on our interpretation of the existing research, offered little support for the continued use of either the ITPA-related diagnostic procedures or the remedial materials. Although we have attempted to evaluate the literature objectively, we recognize the fact that our opinions may evoke varying degrees of opposition among those professionals who currently advocate the use of various psycholinguistic assessment devices and training programs.

In the interest of fairness and because we are cognizant of the important implications this information has for educators, we feel that representative alternate positions should be included in this book. Consequently, we have secured rebuttals and/or statements of position from Dr. Wilma Jo Bush, coauthor of *Aids to Psycholinguistic Teaching* and *Diagnosing Learning Disorders,* Dr. Esther Minskoff, the principal author of the Minskoff, Wiseman, and Minskoff *Program for Developing Language Abilities,* a psycholinguistic training program, and Dr. John McLeod, author of numerous articles about the ITPA and a long-time advocate of psycholinguistic approaches in education.

These individuals are well equipped to react to our presentations and interpretations as well as to offer alternate points of view. Dr. Bush, who completed her doctorate in special education at Texas Tech University, is at the present time an Associate Professor in Education at West Texas State University. Dr. Minskoff, who obtained her Ph.D. in special education from Yeshiva University, has served as an Associate Professor of Special Education at Southern Connecticut University and is currently an independent educational consultant in Virginia. Dr. McLeod, who earned his doctorate in psychology from the University of Queensland, Australia, is presently the Director of the Institute of Child Guidance and Development and Head of the Department for the Education of Exceptional Children at the University of Saskatchewan.

Psycholinguistic Remediation
in the Schools

Wilma Jo Bush

Not chaos-like together crush'd and
 brus'd,
But as the world, harmoniously con-
 fus'd:
Where order in variety we see,
And where, though all things differ, all
 agree.

—Alexander Pope, "Windsor Forest"

When one is faced with the responsibility of assisting in the process of guiding the remedial education of children/youth who are
not achieving satisfactorily in learning the basic skills of reading,
writing, and arithmetic, one is confronted with the decision of
choosing the most appropriate methodology. What path should be
pursued? We ask why the individuals did not learn by the methods
which served others so satisfactorily. We also recognize that there
are many systems to which the majority of children respond with
ease and that our choices of these systems are influenced by personal vantage points of perception and experience.

Just as there are many routes to a central place in a city, there are
many approaches to teaching reading, writing, spelling, and arithmetic. If one has been trained to place the emphasis on the *nature
of language*, one may use the Initial Teaching Alphabet, Color
Coded Systems, or a linguistic approach. If one has been trained to
place the emphasis on the *learner*, one may choose a language
experience approach, programmed readers, or individualized reading. Then if one has been trained in the use of basal readers, one
will likely choose either a specific phonics series, or one that begins
with a whole word approach. Children have been learning to read
well by each of these; that is, the majority of children have and
continue to learn by these presentations. It seems axiomatic that
should one set up experimental designs and teach children to read
using all methods mentioned, no significant differences would be
found among them.

Some few children do not learn by the common modes. The incidence of those who do not is said to be about 3 percent at the least
and 7 percent at the most (Kirk, 1972) depending on the degree of

the problem involved as they are identified through diagnosis and teacher reports. As educators, doctors, and psychologists sought to find reasons for the "non-learner," the terms underachiever, dyslexia, dyscalculia, word blindness, along with many others came into common use. As the pressure grew for educational remediation and the growing variety of identifying terms increased, different experimental approaches, though not necessarily apartheid systems, have become nationally known. The lack of unity in the use of identifying terms and the varieties of remediation techniques have added to the confusion of the individual who faces the responsibility of helping the handicapped person stabilize at satisfactory levels of achievement.

HISTORICAL ASPECTS OF REMEDIATION AND ASSESSMENT

Prior to 1950 there was a paucity of material, direction, or information regarding the remediation of learning problems. There were many identifying terms; but, not only was there disagreement in the use of these, there also were no well-accepted, systematic procedures to assessment which could lead to appropriate remediation.

In the early 1950s help for children who were lagging behind in learning the basic skills was still difficult to obtain. The theory regarding cause and effect relationships dealt largely with the concept of emotional disturbance as a consequence of poor parental management. Some few clinics throughout the nation provided therapy in the form of play and drama activities. The writer was assigned to such a clinic where games structured to insure some success for the clients and where drama activities structured for children to work through their problems were a major part of the therapy. The children involved had been referred by schools and parents largely because of failure to learn to read. The prevailing policy of the clinic was to engage in play and drama for fifty minutes and in remedial reading ten minutes for every hour of therapy. The latter was chosen, not because it was felt to be as beneficial as the play therapy, but because it likely would satisfy the parents who might not understand the practice of play as a means of remediation. The assumption was that children needed to have an opportunity to work out their feelings to free energy needed for attention to their subjects in school. It was during this time that the works of Strauss and Lehtinen (1947), Strauss and Kephart (1955), and Cruickshank, Bentzen, Ratzebergz, and Tannhauser (1961) were becoming known. The kinesthetic techniques by Fernald (1943) were also being used as a means to remediate learning problems. Though their methodologies were designed to help children who had brain injuries, some of their ideas were used in the clinic with the "emotionally disturbed" children. It was later that the visual perception techniques by Frostig and Horne (1964) were introduced to aid in visual perception and visual motor development.

Concurrently with the work of Strauss and others, Myklebust (1954) was writing on differential diagnosis and Kirk and McCarthy (1961) were busy authoring a test to examine more discrete differences among children who gave evidence of normal aptitudes but who functioned as if they were retarded. It was this test which offered a construct by which one might see differences which were not detected so simply in other tests. As the WISC profile provided a construct which helped one see more clearly the varieties of functions in the Stanford Binet Test, the Illinois Test of Psycholinguistic Abilities provided another construct through which one might view the behavior of children. It can be said of the ITPA what Guilford (1959) said of his Structure of Intellect, "This is only the beginning." Anders (1974) likens this appearance of the ITPA with the famous suborbital flight of John Glenn. How wonderful indeed did his brief downrange flight seem to us. And, then, within years, we were on the moon. As the teacher is pressured for accountability, there is a need for more differentiated means of evaluation and as superordinate tests of the future which build upon the WISC, the Stanford Binet, and the ITPA are authored, one may see more deeply into the functional behavior of individuals of all ages. It is through the use of these tools and others that individualized remediation can be planned without dependence on educated "guesses" only.

REMEDIATION

Remediation is the term used to identify a procedure that seeks to structure materials and stimuli in such a way that children who have specific problems in understanding/comprehension, in memory, in perception, or in conceptual thinking may have a better chance to perceive and interpret correctly the materials before them and remember the content therein. One of the purposes is that the individual will communicate this function to the teacher through the acts of reading, writing, spelling, and working arithmetic.

Remedial education is predicated on the premise that a specific learning problem has a chance of amelioration if the proper approach, time, and continuous effort are provided. Where there is a brain injury, the theory that another area of the brain will become the central receiver, organizer, and controlling force for various functions has long been accepted by authorities in the field of brain pathology. Cerebral palsy treatment throughout the nation has attested to this concept by training motor-impaired, brain-injured individuals to control fine-motor and gross-motor movements. The assumption regarding remediation of perceptual problems is that this same principle is at work when children have shown gains after a variety of techniques of training have been tried.

Whereas the training for control of motor functions has been in existence for several decades, the emphasis on detecting and remediating specific learning disabilities is relatively new. The search for means of helping the academically impaired brain-injured child, the deaf child with language impairment as well as hearing loss, and the pseudo-mentally retarded child have led to the focus on remedial education. The continued pressures for accountability are forcing all educators to take a close look at remedial methodology and the learning of the basic skills.

Traditional Tutoring

Whereas remediation is no new term, it has not been used in the past to identify supplementary educational help. Rather, the term *tutoring* has been commonly employed, and it has denoted a different kind of training than remediation. It has more often followed along the same procedures found in the traditional classroom which have been provided for those children and youth generally slow in subjects matter areas and *not specifically* in single functions, such as in comprehension only or in memory only. Tutoring deals with the act of additional help with *subjects* with which the child/adolescent is having specific difficulty. The child begins to fail reading, for example, and a person, usually a retired teacher, is employed to guide the individual in a review of the difficult letters and words on a daily or tri-weekly basis. The standard pattern is to secure the school text, if possible, and give the pupil the individual help which too often is not provided during the school day because of the large numbers of children in the classrooms. When the school text cannot be acquired, another text is used as a guide, and the tutoring continues as the child experiences another, but likely similar method of learning to read. In traditional tutoring, the teacher-tutor moves from the academic subject to linguistic and psycholinguistic activities (figure 4). The activities are approached without psycholinguistic and linguistic plan and order, but the tutor cannot escape

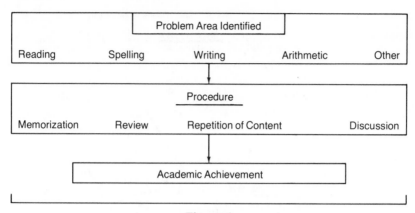

Figure 4
Theoretical Construct for Traditional Tutoring

the use of these if she uses words or gestures. A child is receiving verbal input, comprehending verbal input, and expressing verbally in any teaching situation. Hyman (1974) points this out succinctly as he quotes Smith's statement, "Teaching cannot occur without the use of language. Teaching is above all, a linguistic activity."

Such an accidental relationship to linguistics cannot provide the direction that is needed. A construct such as a psycholinguistic approach not only provides this direction but also provides for more creativity as can be seen in the following discussion.

Psycholinguistic Remediation

Psycholinguistics, as a word can readily be recognized as an extension of the word linguistic. Webster's dictionary defines linguistics as the study of human speech including the units, nature, structure, and modification of language. Overlooking the slang expression, *psycho,* the prefix, according to Dorland's Medical Dictionary, denotes a relationship to the psyche or to the mind. Thus, one might conclude that at least one dimension of psycholinguistics is that study of the way the mind processes language. The other dimensions deal with the sensory channels used in processing language and the automatic and representational levels of function.

It is not difficult to understand a construct for psycholinguistic operations, but it is difficult to isolate a remediation procedure from the construct into a hardline methodology *not* found in traditional tutoring. The psycholinguistic construct does give one a base for planning remediation when it is apparent that a child/adolescent is

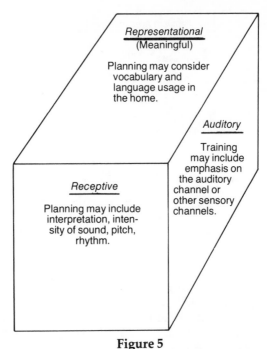

Figure 5
Dimensional Construct for Beginning Remediation
(Auditory-Receptive-Representational)

failing subjects in school. Such remediation plans have been shown to be viable models in individual cases, though some studies using groups of students have not shown conclusive results! An examination of the complexities of psycholinguistic methodology vs. traditional methodology illuminates the problem and provides some answers.

As the possibility of multidimensional aspects in the learning process are considered, admission would have to be made that any construct to begin remediation is just that—a beginning. For example, if in one case the scores from the Illinois Test of Psycholinguistic Abilities strongly substantiates an auditory receptive problem, then the remediator using the psycholinguistic approach would begin a process of diagnostic teaching using many diverse ideas to try to find an inroad to learning. Figure 5 shows the possibilities of experimentation which include not only meaningfulness of content but also differences in intensity of sound, pitch, and rhythm, as well as the vocabulary of the individual. Figure 6 shows the global possibilities of a multidimensional construct using the ITPA. The term

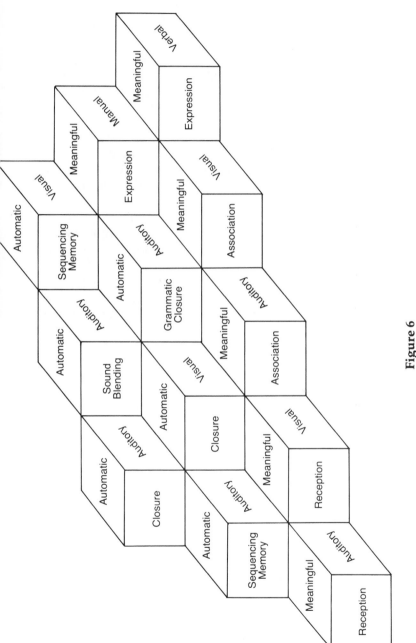

Figure 6
*Multidimensional Construct of the Illinois Test of
Psycholinguistic Abilities*

91

meaningful is substituted for the term representational to identify the representational level.

To add to the complexity of proceeding with remediation, the remediator may see within the established plan of some teaching method another means of attacking the problem. For example, after finding that a child, failing in reading, is also diagnosed as having an auditory receptive problem, a remediator may choose to provide more experiences for discrimination of sounds and words by using the Gillingham-Stillman (1965) system of teaching. The expectancy might be that the child would eventually develop word attack skills which would subsequently result in reading improvement if a consistent and repetitious presentation of phonics were employed. Another remediator might choose, considering the same diagnosis, that an individual should have a chance to learn to read through a sensory channel other than the deficit one (identified as auditory, in this case). She might choose to bombard the child with a flashcard approach, which entailed a combination of kinesthetic and visual stimulation. In both cases the formats would be classified under the psycholinguistic construct because they both deal with the units and the structure of language and they both deal with inputs or sensory channels, *but* they would not be identical methods of remediation. This is to emphasize the fact that once one has looked at a child through the "lens" of the Illinois test it is not likely that any single unitary psycholinguistic method of remediation will be found though the remediation were planned after the ITPA construct. At this time probably no standard approach is being followed in psycholinguistic remediation. There are individual cases describing efforts using the psycholinguistic approach (see case examples on p. 93) and there are activities to follow, Kirk and Kirk (1971) and Bush and Giles (1969), but no step-by-step methodology. The MWM (Minskoff, Wiseman, and Minskoff, 1972) series does offer a developmental approach, as do the Peabody Developmental Language Kits, but where remediation is considered, the psycholinguistic procedure is very likely a loosely knit methodology influenced by the perceptual set of the individual remediator. This can be an asset to remediation, but what appears to be needed, if we are to get valid results from research, is a set of guidelines from which a remediator may find avenues for diversity while staying within well-defined limits of the construct. This would simplify the process of controlling for variables.

Examples of Individual Cases

As both psychologist and educational diagnostician the writer has used the Illinois Test of Psycholinguistic Abilities since the first month of the experimental edition and has found it to be a very useful tool in a battery of tests, helping to highlight strengths and weaknesses in children who are failing in school. No two cases are ever alike and likely never should have exactly the same recommendations for remediation. Case after case can be cited where improvement has occurred using different procedures when profiles were quite similar. The two cases which follow are examples of cases with similar profiles from the ITPA, but with several factors determining the direction of the remedial education. In each case it was the ITPA construct that provided the basic clue toward methodology.

Case I.

One child had failed reading during his first grade year and had become inattentive and discouraged. He was brought to me for evaluation during his last month of the school year. The findings showed that he did have normal intelligence but that he could not read though he appeared ready to learn. The ITPA was the one test in the battery which brought into focus a specific area of weakness. In most of the auditory subtests he showed a significant difference when compared with the visual subtests. The decision was made to keep him in the first grade and to tutor him during the summer with a visual presentation method. (The school which he attended taught only a phonics approach.) The mother left my office with mimeographed sheets of activities to follow. These were commensurate with first grade interests and capacities and followed the ITPA format of the process of learning, emphasizing the visual channel activities. The mother, who was a certified teacher, tutored the child and by fall he had started to read. She kept up the specific tutoring for over a year when she began to see signs that he was able to continue without her help. This boy is now in junior high school and is making good grades.

Case II.

Case two was a boy, also in the first grade, who never completed his school work according to the teacher. She averred that they were on good terms, that he was quiet and obedient, but that he never seemed to know what he was supposed to do. The parents had reported normal auditory acuity, but had added that the child often did not follow directions as given. The psychological evaluation showed normal intelligence, and it also showed that he was achieving at his grade level expectancy. The findings from the ITPA revealed significant auditory channel weaknesses. The main reason for referral was to determine whether he should be kept in the first grade for another year. I could not recommend this on the basis of the achievement findings from the test battery. I discussed the matter with the teacher, whom I knew to speak in soft tones in her classroom. Though there was no acuity problem reported, there was obviously some problem in his ability or habit of listening and interpreting. My recommendation in this matter was not tutoring. He had learned to read, write, spell, and work arithmetic. He did not follow directions from the teacher or the parents and often had not interpreted what was said to him, whether unconscious, conscious, or incapable. This observation was borne out later by his Scout Master, who had not agreed with me earlier about the diagnosis. It was decided to place him in a room with a teacher who projected her voice in a forceful way and that always both parent and teacher would follow-up any directions given by ascertaining that he had understood. Whatever the cause, and at that time it was not possible to explore further because of the circumstances, the boy did begin to show improvement in school. He, too, is now a junior high school student and his father reports that he had no trouble completing his work after that year. His father's words were, "he's not the *A* student, but he does not fail and he does his work independently."

Psycholinguistic Remediation Guidelines

A systematic plan for remediation must begin with a format. A systematic psycholinguistic plan could follow two well-known constructs, the ITPA, and the other, a construct defined by Johnson and Myklebust (1967). Both of these are found within figure 7, a Format for Psycholinguistic Remediation. The relationship between the two is not shown but it can readily be seen that one can encompass the other by examining the terminology used in classifying the language functions.

The format, as identified in figure 7, provides an overview of the procedure to follow in remediation:

1. The problem is first identified, e.g., reading.
2. Psycholinguistic constructs for remediation procedure are explored. In this case either the Myklebust or Kirk-McCarthy constructs are suggested.
3. Subject matter content from the basic skill area (reading or other) is chosen.
4. The specific subject matter material is presented through a psycholinguistic procedure described on p. 96.

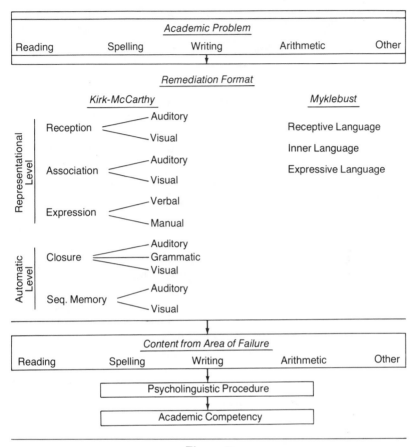

Figure 7
Format for Psycholinguistic Remediation

If psycholinguistic remediation proceeds without consideration of the specific basic skill weakness and the subject matter therein, the expectancy outcomes would likely be more general in nature. These general outcomes would likely be:

1. Greater receptivity to words and ideas through listening and attending;
2. Increased capacity to relate meaning of events and ideas;
3. Enhanced skills in using proper syntax and grammatic sequences;

4. Increased speed of visual perception, recognition of wholes from viewing only parts;
5. Increased capacity to remember the sequence of shapes, figures, letters, and numbers.

The general outcomes provide a base for improvement in the cognitive skills but to complete the psycholinguistic remediation plan one must include specific subject-matter-content material. The specific objectives in remediation are rarely to achieve general outcomes only. It is for this reason when using a psycholinguistic plan, one must first begin with an analysis of the diagnostic information including achievement levels showing the basic skill weaknesses. There would be no need for remediation unless some weaknesses were identified. Following this step the remediator should consider (1) the aspects of sensory channels of learning, (2) the meaningfulness of the material presented, and (3) the process involved.

As the remediator examines the dimensions of sensory channel, level of representation, and process, the decision must be made whether to follow the procedure of strengthening the weakest sensory channel in hopes of steady gains in improvement, or to utilize the strongest sensory channel expecting (1) transcoding functions from one modality to another (Jastak and Jastak, 1965), (2) one process to aid another process, or (3) one specific function to become more automatic in nature. Once this decision is made, the remediator may move through a procedure emphasizing either the auditory or the visual modality of learning. In both cases the kinesthetic sensory modality may be used as a reinforcement if it is determined that such a multisensory approach is feasible with the client. In some cases a multisensory approach may cause the neurological system to become "overloaded" and confusion could result.

The following example using *reading* shows the steps to follow when one chooses to plan remediation through the psycholinguistic construct according to Kirk and McCarthy.

Reception process
Show the word, say the word, feel the shape of the word.

Association process
Discuss the meaning of similar words and similarities and differences of words, both by sight and sound.

Expression process

Talk about words, express ideas about words and if the words deal with concrete objects, give child ample opportunity to discuss.

Closure process

Use words in sentences in a variety of ways (work on syntax). Look at words and allow for tracing, completion of incomplete words. Say incomplete words and let child guess what one is saying.

Memory process

Place words in a line in a prescribed order; disarrange order and allow child to rearrange in the original order. Say words in prescribed order. Allow child to repeat in the same order.

The important principles to follow in the use of the procedure would be to (1) keep the content consistent from classroom to resource room where remediation occurs—the techniques and activities may vary but the content should remain the same as the content to which the child is exposed in the classroom, (2) do not ask the child to read or respond without clues or help, and (3) consider the needs of the child in relation to the temperament of the teacher-remediator.

Principle No. 3 is an often overlooked principle which is of critical importance. McKeachie and Doyle (1966) have reported that there is a relationship between the needs of the child and the temperament of the teacher. A child with a need for power does much better in a situation where he has opportunity to express himself freely. A child with a need for affiliation (to be accepted) tends to do better under a teacher who takes a personal interest in him, and he does the poorest when the teacher is remote and distant. Conversely, where students are low in need for affiliation, they do better when the teacher remains remote. Where students have a need for achievement, results appear to be more puzzling. These students appear to do very well when no pressure is placed on them, but the minute the pressure is applied, they begin to lose motivation. They appear to get the greatest satisfaction from achieving for themselves without being pressed into it by frequent quizzes and by being told whether or not they are doing well. Students who are low in the need for achievement appear more motivated and learn more when the teacher maintains pressure on them to achieve.

The important point is that the effect of what the teacher-tutor does depends upon many variables and among them is the needs of the student with whom the teacher is dealing. Anxiety, need for approval, ability to delay satisfaction until a better job can be done, and ability to see relationship between what the student does and what the teacher is approving are all factors influencing the motivation of an individual in a remediation session.

For the ultimate in remediation to occur a recognition of the needs of the pupil on the part of the teacher and an acceptance of the teacher's behavior on the part of the pupil must be attained. Given these conditions and no absolute physiological blocks to learning, significant gains should increase in proportion to the expertise of the remediator.

Research and Remediation

Important in educational remediation are some major facts which have a bearing on research. One of these is that remediation is a highly individualized procedure, which may not show the strength of its effect among total scores from studies on groups. A child may be making improvement individually, but he may be the only one in a group who is showing significant gains and his scores may not be weighted sufficiently to show a change in the total group score.

A second aspect which overlaps somewhat with the first, but which may be discussed individually is that no two learning problems are sufficiently alike to take scores from group of "non-readers," for example, and compare them with scores obtained from a system of teaching. Bush (1965) found that some individuals having difficulty learning (most of them had been dropouts in school) tended to do better under certain conditions and presentations than under others. Myklebust (1967) and Boden (1973) both speak of visual dyslexia and auditory dyslexia, and Boden further identifies these as dyseidetic and dysphonetic problems in reading. To examine reasons for these differences let us look at some conclusions regarding focal brain lesions. Only a few facts relative to auditory disturbances are mentioned here. Luria (1965) reports on the analysis and synthesis of operations in brain pathology and states that among brain injured individuals if the damage occurs in specific areas of the brain, the ability to hear sound blends is disturbed and if the damage occurs in another position, only the ability to hear phonemes is disturbed. Other problems can occur between "correlative" or "oppositional" phonemes, i.e., phonemes which differ from one another by a single distinctive feature as in sounds of /d/ and /t/, /b/ and /p/, and /z/ and /s/. As a result it can become impossible for a person to form differential conditioned reflexes to different speech sounds. He then points out many other differences in the problem of perception of sound. It is possible for severe disturbance of phonemic hearing to be accompanied by preservation of musical perception. Such persons with severe forms of sensory aphasia are often able to recognize and produce familiar melodies. Conversely there may be adequate phonemic hearing, yet the individual may not recognize or remember musical sounds. The two functions appear superficially to be related, but the dissociation serves as an example of the varied differences in the process of brain mechanisms which psychologically appear to be essentially identical.

Though these differences reported by Luria are related to specific brain injury, the concept of maturational lag, another cause for learning disabilities (Bender, 1958), could well suggest that the dynamics might be the same in terms of the freedom of analysis and synthesis. At least, in this, one can see the individuality and complexity of learning particularly when the process is disturbed.

One can also question the validity of conclusions drawn from any research which compares "learning" scores with subtest scores as on the ITPA. A subtest may not be differentiated enough to identify a total remediation approach for an individual or a group, but it may support other information which can provide for differential remediation. The value of a diagnostic tool in the hands of a good clinician must not be overlooked.

The third point is that normally one does not expect phenomenal gains in a hurry. The child involved generally has had many months and sometimes years of failure. For messages, as in reading, to be transcoded by intersensory cooperations is a difficult and complex task. Jastak and Jastak (1965) emphasize this by stating that reading disability is by far the most numerous and most insidious of all learning defects and that such a disability does not yield easily to any known treatment. Thus one does not treat a child for two or three months or for that matter, a year, and expect "cures."

Another related point regarding the use of treatment with large numbers of children is that children who are successful in academics, linguistics, or psycholinguistics and who are socially and self-adjusted likely will not show significant gains after "treatment."

What children have learned well will not likely be exceeded significantly with bombardment of a new technique. Remediation is for
children who need help in learning, and until we have teaching
systems to meet the needs of *all* children and tools of evaluation
complete enough to measure for the needs of *all* children, we will
need to continue to use a variety of techniques and a variety of tests.

The writer makes these recommendations for research of the future:

1. Before comparing scores from "non-readers," e.g., with any
   subtest scores on the ITPA, determine whether the children
   are dysphonetic or dyseidetic; then compare dysphonetic
   function with the auditory test scores and the dyseidetic
   function with the visual subtest scores. Medical research of
   the future will have to provide means for determining the
   intrasensory differences of sensory channels of learning. At
   present we must be satisfied with only a few visual processes
   vs. auditory processes in this context.
2. Control for *linguistic variables* in traditional teaching if it is to
   be compared to psycholinguistic teaching and remediation.
3. Provide longitudinal studies of individual cases, not groups
   of children. Also control for modification of the procedure as
   the remediation proceeds.
4. Control for needs of children and temperament of the remediator.
5. Control for individuality in completed research when making
   comparisons with other research. Do not "lump" different
   research together as if it were all alike.

Response to Dr. Bush's Viewpoint

In the initial sections of her discussion, Dr. Wilma Jo Bush outlines
the plight of teachers who are faced with the day-to-day management
and instruction of children failing in school and describes briefly the
development of the interest in remediating the problems of these
children. The point is made early that the ITPA was developed so that
professionals could accurately document the presence of psycholinguistic abilities and weaknesses in children. We, of course,
have no quarrel with the purposes for which the ITPA, or any other
standardized test for that matter, may have been constructed; in fact,
we feel that perhaps Kirk's greatest contribution to American special
education may well prove to be the support he has given to the

importance of considering "intraindividual" differences (see chapter 2). We do question, however, whether the ITPA can be used with confidence as a valid measure of those intraindividual differences which have relevance for school success. Our reasons for this opinion are based squarely on the interpretation of the studies discussed in chapter 3.

Also, we do not accept as valid Dr. Bush's application of Guilford's 1959 statement, "This is only the beginning" to the ITPA. The ITPA has been available commercially since 1961; literally hundreds of research studies have utilized the instrument; and yet, after all this, the value of the test for educational purposes remains essentially unsubstantiated.

In the remainder of the discussion, Dr. Bush gives her orientation to the remediation of learning disabilities, especially those pertaining to psycholinguistics. This section is particularly useful for readers who may be unfamiliar with the assumptions underlying psycholinguistic remediation and the application of ITPA-related assessment and constructs to instructional practice. Throughout this section, examples are provided where the major theoretical constructs of the ITPA—modality, level of meaningfulness, and process—are used for the purpose of either evaluating pupils or selecting training activities for them. We recognize and wish to point out that Dr. Bush makes some statements with which other psycholinguistically oriented educators might disagree, but we feel that the clinical approach which is outlined in her discussion is fairly representative.

To us, such approaches appear to be decidedly deductive in nature, a characteristic of most clinical orientations. However, as is the case with all deductive systems, philosophical or educational, this particular psycholinguistic approach is entirely dependent upon the validity of its fundamental postulates. In this case, no matter how pleasing the vocabulary, how reassuring the structure, how comforting the activities, or how intellectually interesting the concepts may be for the clinician-teacher, there comes the time when one must ask the question: Are the ITPA subtests and dimensions, and by inference the constructs for which they stand, really instructionally useful components of academic success? Even a cursory examination of the material included in chapter 3 should be sufficient to stimulate at least some degree of doubt in the minds of the most ardent advocates of psycholinguistic training.

Dr. Bush concludes with a series of recommendations regarding future research. Expectedly, since she is a clinically oriented professional, Dr. Bush emphasizes the need for studies of individual cases rather than for additional studies using groups of subjects. Our opinions on this topic have already been presented at the end of chapter 4. However, several additional points can be made. First, we do agree that N-of-one research, case studies, etc., have a useful place in educational research but they too have serious shortcomings when employed to validate training procedures. For example, the subjects invariably improve with the passage of time regardless of treatment or lack of treatment. Second, it is surprising to read that advocates of psycholinguistic training shun group research on the basis that it is difficult to match the experimental and control children on the critical dimensions, for one of the assumptions that most of them make, including Dr. Bush, is that psycholinguistic differences among children, even subtle ones, are readily identifiable through the use of "a diagnostic tool in the hands of a good clinician. . . ." If this is indeed the case, then there is little reason why group designs should be avoided. In short, if the measurement expertise exists to "diagnose" children on the basis of the ITPA-related constructs and/or to distinguish between "dysphonetic" and "dyseidetic" children for the purposes of implementing "appropriate" teaching, why can't the same procedures be used to match children for research purposes? Other points made by Dr. Bush regarding research designs have been incorporated into our response to Dr. Minskoff.

Research on the Efficacy of Remediating
Psycholinguistic Disabilities:
Critique and Recommendations

Esther H. Minskoff

The review of research on the ITPA by Newcomer and Hammill makes an important contribution to the field of learning disabilities because it focuses on critical issues, particularly that of the efficacy of training psycholinguistic disabilities. However, their analysis of thirty–nine studies on the efficacy of psycholinguistic training has resulted in some oversimplified conclusions and faulty implications. The question underlying their analysis has been: "Is psycholinguistic training effective?" A more productive approach for such an analysis should be based on the question, "What types of remedial methods are most effective with what kinds of learning disabled children under what conditions?" Because of their oversimplified approach, they have grouped together thirty–nine studies with non-comparable subjects and non-comparable treatments. Moreover, they have reviewed mostly methodologically inadequate studies in which there was short-term training using general approaches to treatment primarily with mentally retarded or disadvantaged children having no diagnosed learning disabilities. Principles and practices in the field of learning disabilities indicate that there is, or should be, long-term training using specific approaches to treatment with non-retarded children having diagnosed learning disabilities.

In the first section of my contribution there is a critique of Newcomer and Hammill's approach to reviewing these efficacy studies. The second section deals with underlying assumptions and variables to be described and controlled in all efficacy studies; while the final section includes a discussion of past, present, and future directions in the field of psycholinguistic training.

REVIEW OF ITPA TRAINING STUDIES

In their analysis of thirty–nine studies on remediation in which the ITPA was used, Newcomer and Hammill have compared studies which differ markedly, or are inadequate, in three major respects: the nature of the subjects, the treatment, and the experimental design. In effect, they have made an "apples and pears" comparison.

Nature of the Subjects

The nature of the subjects used in each of these thirty–nine studies was radically different from one to the other. Moreover, the subjects used in most of these studies were not representative of the bulk of the learning disabled population ordinarily diagnosed and served in the schools. The subjects in these studies varied in the three following ways: (1) whether or not they were learning disabled, (2) the nature of their learning disabilities, and (3) background characteristics.

1. *Learning disabled vs. non-learning disabled subjects.*   It is not apparent from Newcomer and Hammill's analysis whether the subjects in these thirty–nine studies were learning disabled. Fifteen of the studies used either educable or trainable mentally retarded children. The most widely accepted definition of learning disabilities excludes the mentally retarded.* Using this definition, the subjects in these studies would not be considered learning disabled. Even if a definition encompassing the retarded were used, there is no indication that all of these retarded subjects had learning disabilities. Practically all of the learning disabled children served in the schools are of average intelligence; therefore, generalizations from these studies to the learning disabled population are quite limited.

In most, if not all, of the thirty–one studies in which a general approach to treatment was taken, there was no analysis of each subject's profile of learning characteristics. Therefore, it is possible that a large number of subjects in these studies did not, in fact, have learning disabilities. In these studies, heterogeneous groups of non-learning disabled children as well as children with different types of psycholinguistic disabilities were given the same treatment. Such a group approach masks any positive results of remediation for specific kinds of children.

Subjects who do not have learning disabilities in particular psycholinguistic areas who are given treatment to develop these areas will not show any sizable improvement. This is a logical as-

---

*Children with special (specific) learning disabilities exhibit a disorder in one or more of the basic psychological processes involved in understanding or in using spoken or written language. These may be manifested in disorders of listening, thinking, talking, reading, writing, spelling, or arithmetic. They include conditions which have been referred to as perceptual handicaps, brain injury, minimal brain dysfunction, dyslexia, developmental aphasia, etc. They do not include learning problems which are due primarily to visual, hearing, or motor handicaps, to mental retardation, emotional disturbance, or to environmental disadvantage. (Title VI-A, Elementary and Secondary Education Act Annual Reports for 1968. U.S.O.E., April, 1969).

sumption in that such subjects are already functioning at or near their current capacities in these psycholinguistic areas. Generalizations from such studies cannot be made to children who have learning disabilities and who do have room for substantial improvement in their disability areas.

2. *Nature of the learning disabilities.* Because the learning disabled are a heterogeneous population, research with such children must provide data on the type, severity, and whenever possible, the causation of the learning disabilities. Although Newcomer and Hammill recognize that given methods may be effective with subjects having certain characteristics, they have not analyzed the thirty–nine studies in relationship to these subject variables.

In studies where learning disabled subjects were used, children with different areas of psycholinguistic disabilities were given the same treatment (e.g., a child with an Auditory Reception disability and another with a Visual Closure disability might both have been given the same PLDK stimulation). Such children require varying training programs tailored to their specific disability areas.

Even children with disabilities in the same psycholinguistic area may vary in their specific behavioral symptoms. For example, two children may have disabilities in Auditory Reception, but one may have difficulty only in understanding lengthy materials as lectures, while the other may have difficulty only with discriminating speech sounds. Obviously, each of these children requires a different remedial program.

It is axiomatic that the more severe the learning disability, the more impervious it is to successful remediation; and yet there was no attention given to this important variable in Newcomer and Hammill's review.

There was also no consideration in the review of the causation of the subjects' psycholinguistic disabilities. Although it is difficult, and in some cases impossible, to isolate the cause of a child's disability, such information is, nevertheless, pertinent to any research on psycholinguistic training. Disabilities associated with constitutional factors (e.g., genetic or neurological), in all probability, are more difficult to remediate than disabilities due to environmental factors (e.g., poor teaching). Therefore, the absence of a case history approach, in which there is an attempt to identify the probable cause of each subject's disability, results in groups of subjects who may respond differentially to remediation.

3. *Background characteristics.* The subjects in these thirty–nine studies varied with respect to IQ, age, total profile of learning

abilities and disabilities, social class, and race. The limitations of using retarded subjects whose mastery of remedial learnings is constricted by virtue of their retardation was discussed above.

Newcomer and Hammill report that studies with preschoolers showed significant improvement in Auditory Association, while those with elementary level children found Verbal and Manual Expression to be areas of growth. These findings have little meaning unless they are related to the specific nature of the subjects' disabilities at each age level and the corresponding remediation given.

Differing results should be obtained for remediation at various age levels because qualitatively different populations of subjects are involved and because the school and social demands for psycholinguistic performance change with age. Children diagnosed as learning disabled at the preschool level usually have difficulties mastering developmental tasks, such as running; while children so identified at the elementary level most often have academic difficulties. Many learning disabled children diagnosed at the elementary level did not exhibit significant problems prior to school. Therefore, preschoolers diagnosed as learning disabled have different types of difficulties than elementary level children, and frequently, are more severely disabled. Moreover, the school and social demands on the preschooler differ from those made on the elementary level child; therefore, the nature of the remediation given each should vary, making direct comparisons between them difficult.

In addition, it seems that an emotional overlay often becomes associated with a child's disability as he grows older. A child with such a problem tends to avoid performing tasks involving his disability area. This complicates the success of any remedial method with children as they grow older.

No consideration was given by Newcomer and Hammill to the subjects' areas of psycholinguistic ability. These are as important as disability areas because they are frequently used as aids in remediation, and because they may provide the means by which children can independently compensate for their disabilities.

In eighteen of the thirty–nine studies, disadvantaged or lower class subjects were used. Some of the eighteen studies evaluated the efficacy of Head Start types of compensatory programs blanketly developed for an entire group. Such studies should not then have been included in the review of research on the efficacy of remediation of specific psycholinguistic disabilities.

The studies in which race was considered, for the most part, involved lower class children as most of the racial groups were disadvantaged. Stereotyping of learning characteristics of an entire race is not possible; and thus, any general program based on such stereotypes does not involve remediation of specific disabilities. The implications from general treatment studies using lower class or racial groups are not applicable to the vast majority of the learning disabled in the schools.

Nature of the Treatment

Newcomer and Hammill made the assumption that the treatments in all thirty-nine studies were comparable because they analyzed the entire group of studies on the basis of whether a majority showed positive results. Such an analysis is not appropriate because the treatments in these studies were non-comparable inasmuch as they varied in four major respects: content, time factors, group vs. individual treatment, and the teacher variable. They should have made an individual analysis of the treatment given for each psycholinguistic area in each of the thirty–nine studies. Then it would have been possible to group studies with like treatment variables, and thus, identify those specific remedial methods that resulted in improvement in each psycholinguistic area, and those that did not.

Content of treatment. In thirty-one of the thirty-nine studies there was a general, nonindividualized approach in which there was no relationship between the treatment given and the children's psycholinguistic disabilities. One of the most established principles, and hopefully practices, for treating children with learning disabilities is to fit the remediation directly to children's specific learning disabilities. Obviously, this was not done in these thirty-one studies; and hence, they cannot be considered appropriate treatment studies.

In sixteen of the thirty-nine studies, the PLDK, a developmental, not remedial, program for general language stimulation was used. This program does not provide systematic training for each of the twelve language areas of the ITPA. Thus, remediation of a child's specific disability could not have been provided in these studies.

The content of the treatment in each of these thirty–nine studies varied tremendously. For example, Painter (1966) used sensory-motor training based on the works of Barsch and Kephart. As expected, she obtained significant results for Manual Expression, but not for most of the other psycholinguistic areas. There is no logical reason to expect areas such as Grammatic Closure to improve with such training, and yet Newcomer and Hammill interpret Painter's findings as not supporting psycholinguistic training. Furthermore, her treatment should not be grouped with other studies in which such sensory-motor training was not given.

Only eight of the thirty–nine studies utilized an individualized approach, and yet even in these eight, there was great variability. In some cases it is virtually impossible to determine the content of the remediation provided. For example, in the Spollen and Ballif study (1971), it is only reported that activities and materials based on the works of Kephart, Montessori, Frostig, Fernald, and Barsch were used. From such a vague description it is impossible to trace any resulting changes in the subjects' performances to certain teaching methods; and furthermore, it is not possible to replicate such treatment in subsequent research.

Training of seven of the twelve psycholinguistic areas of the ITPA involves auditory or verbal disabilities. This form of training is the most difficult to describe and control because the vehicle through which it is presented is the teacher-pupil verbal interaction. Although the MWM Program gives specific teaching strategies and scripts for such training (Minskoff, Wiseman, and Minskoff, 1972) and Minskoff (1974) has described a framework for using verbal interaction for treating different types of auditory and verbal disabilities, the teacher is still the major determinant of such training. To assess the efficacy of training auditory and verbal disabilities, it is necessary to record the teacher's interactions with her students so they can be analyzed. Obviously, none of these thirty–nine studies, most of which involved auditory and verbal training, even approached such an analysis.

All efficacy studies must attempt to provide as detailed and specific a description of the content of the remediation as possible. However, even with MWM Program (which has not yet been the subject of efficacy studies), in which there are systematic, comprehensive activities and materials for remediating each of the twelve ITPA areas, there is still much latitude for variability. This stems from how the teacher fits the many activities and materials to each child's specific disability; how she goes beyond the basic materials provided and creates additional materials; and her competency as the controller of the remedial teaching act.

The research on remediation of psycholinguistic disabilities continually will be plagued by problems of comparability of content. However, to a considerable extent, it is possible to overcome many of these problems by designing and analyzing efficacy studies on the basis of the fifteen criteria described in the next section.

Time factors. The thirty-nine efficacy studies varied on time factors. In fifteen studies, less than fifty hours of treatment was given, while in the remainder more than fifty was given. At first glance, fifty hours seems like a considerable amount of time; however, it becomes negligible when compared to the hundreds or even thousands of hours required for mastery of various academic and social learnings without the handicap of psycholinguistic disabilities. If the goal of remediation is to train a child to master learnings that he has not been able to master by traditional methods over a number of years in the past, it is unlikely, as Newcomer and Hammill recognize, that any of these studies provided adequate time for mastery.

Individual vs. group treatment. One of the most crucial aspects involves whether remediation was given on an individual, small group, or large group basis. Newcomer and Hammill did not consider this factor in their analysis. The results of individual remediation cannot be generalized to those of group remediation, and results with small groups are not directly applicable to large groups.

When individual remediation is given, the teacher interacts 100 percent of the time with one child. Assuming that the teacher equally divides her attention among all children in a group, she interacts 25 percent of the time with each child in a small group of four, and only 5 percent in a large group of twenty. It cannot be assumed that when a teacher is not directly interacting with one particular child, that he is learning from her interactions with others. To add further complexity, the time factor is related to the group factor. Long-term training with a large group may not have the same results as short-term training with the same methods on an individual basis.

Teacher variables. Probably the foremost factor involved in efficacy studies is whether the teachers are implementing the remedial treatment under investigation in the way that it should be. However, no consideration was given to this factor by Newcomer and Hammill.

Teacher variables such as the degree of training and the amount of experience with the learning disabled are also factors that may be related to the success of a particular remedial treatment.

Experimental Design

Although Newcomer and Hammill recognized that many of these thirty-nine studies contained methodological errors, they still accepted and interpreted the results of these studies. Since each of these thirty–nine studies included one or more of the following methodological errors, their results must be viewed with extreme caution.

1. Subjects came from different populations than the population to be investigated (i.e., the learning disabled).
2. Heterogeneous subjects were combined into groups that should have been homogeneous.
3. Inadequate data were used for the diagnosis of psycholinguistic disabilities as well as the evaluation of the training.
4. Groups were not matched on variables relevant to the treatment.
5. There was no randomization of groups.
6. There was no control of the attention factor.
7. There was inadequate description of the treatment.
8. The treatment did not correspond to the treatment to be investigated (i.e., remediation of specific psycholinguistic disabilities).
9. There was biased evaluation because it was not done in the blind.
10. There were no specified criteria for mastery of remedial learnings.

GUIDELINES FOR RESEARCH ON THE EFFICACY OF REMEDIATING PSYCHOLINGUISTIC DISABILITIES

As previously stated, the central question to be answered by research on remediation of psycholinguistic disabilities is: *What types of remedial methods are most effective with what kinds of learning disabled children under what conditions?* Underlying this question are seven assumptions which are discussed below.

Underlying Assumptions

The learning disabled are heterogeneous.   Children with psycholinguistic disabilities constitute a diverse population who can have disabilities in any one or more of the twelve ITPA areas. Even children with disabilities in the same psycholinguistic area may exhibit differing symptoms. Since the learning disabled are heterogeneous, there is no one or even few methods that are best suited for all such children. Rather, the effectiveness of a particular method, to a substantial degree, is determined by its appropriateness to a child's disability area and specific behavioral symptoms.

Psycholinguistic disabilities can be identified. It must be assumed that specific psycholinguistic disabilities can be identified through presently available means. However, the ITPA is not the sole means for such an identification. As Newcomer and Hammill have pointed out, when Kirk et al. constructed a subtest to sample each of the twelve psycholinguistic areas, they had to select one sample of behavior to represent general functioning in that area. It is not known if each subarea sample by the ITPA subtest is the best representation of other subareas. Furthermore, it is not known if there is one best subarea that can be used to represent general functioning because each psycholinguistic area is a complex aggregate of many diverse subareas.

To identify the specific subareas of a psycholinguistic area, it is necessary to analyze the construct, or the meaning, of a psycholinguistic area in relationship to various social and academic demands made upon a child at a particular age. Minskoff et al. have made such an analysis of the subareas for each of the twelve psycholinguistic areas for the three to seven language area level (1972) and another analysis for the seven to eleven level (in preparation). At present, there is no one best analysis of subareas; however, all who work with the ITPA model for diagnostic or remedial purposes must make such an analysis. Eventually there should be some concurrence in the field on a comprehensive model of psycholinguistic functioning with specific subareas for each of the twelve general areas.

To diagnose a child's specific psycholinguistic disability, it is necessary to use various tests, most notably the ITPA, diagnostic teaching, and observation. The final diagnosis of a psycholinguistic disability must reveal the general area of disability, the specific symptoms or subareas, and the level of functioning.

Psycholinguistic disabilities can be trained. If it is assumed that a child's disability cannot be remediated, attempts at remedial treatment will not be made and the child will have certain areas of development in which he has not reached a basic level of competence. This, in turn, prevents him from mastering certain requirements for school and social adjustment.

The previous discussion of the thirty–nine studies reviewed by Newcomer and Hammill should definitively indicate that there is *NO* research support for the conclusion that psycholinguistic disabilities cannot be trained. Furthermore, taking the view that they cannot be remediated leads to a pessimism which may prevent a teacher from even trying to teach a learning disabled child.

Psycholinguistic functioning is related to social and academic learning. Newcomer and Hammill's review of studies in which ITPA functioning was correlated with academic performance does not invalidate this assumption because these studies were marred by errors of oversimplification. In all of these studies only one sub-area of each of the twelve psycholinguistic areas was correlated with global measures of academic performance. As previously stated, there are many different subareas in each of the twelve psycholinguistic areas, and each subarea probably correlates differently with various measures of academic learning.

In addition, these studies used global scores ot reading, spelling, and arithmetic. Each of these scores represents a complex integration of many different abilities. It is doubtful that any one psycholinguistic area can substantially contribute to the total variance of such global scores. To investigate the correlation of psycholinguistic and academic functioning, it is necessary to extricate those aspects of academic learning that seem to be logically related to a specific subarea of psycholinguistic functioning. For example, it is likely that understanding the difference between the consonant blends "stop" vs. "spot" (Auditory Reception) is related to mastery of beginning phonics; while visual memory for sequences of letters (Visual Sequential Memory) is probably related to learning to read by a visual method. However, each of these specific psycholinguistic subareas may not correlate with global reading level scores which are dependent upon a great many different reading skills.

Newcomer and Hammill's review omits consideration of the correlation of psycholinguistic functioning with social learning. The goal of education is not merely to train children in the three R's, but also to train them to become socially competent. Some of the sub-areas of the twelve psycholinguistic areas seem to be related to specific aspects of social learning. For example, understanding inflectional differences as in "Is that great!" vs. "Is that great?" (Auditory Reception) or understanding body language (Visual Reception) should be correlated with logically related aspects of a child's social interactions.

A major criterion for creating or evaluating psycholinguistic training should be its relationship to academic and social learning (Minskoff, 1973). It is illogical to train an area such as Visual Sequential Memory with nonsense words when reading and spelling words a child must master can be used. It is unfortunate that in the past, some psycholinguistic training did, indeed, have content of questionable value; however, presently there seems to be a trend away from this.

In summary, it is preposterous to state that the construct underlying a psycholinguistic area (such as understanding what is heard) is not related to school or social functioning. Rather, the way the construct underlying a psycholinguistic area is measured by the ITPA or trained by a particular remedial method may not be related to academic or social learning.

Future research should explore the critical question of the relationship of psycholinguistic functioning and academic and social learning, but such research must take a complex multivariate approach for correlating specific subareas of psycholinguistic functioning with logically selected specific academic and social behaviors.

Psycholinguistic training differs at various age levels. The nature of the learning disabled children identified at the preschool, elementary, and secondary levels qualitatively differs. Moreover, the academic and social demands made for psycholinguistic performance vary with age, and thus, the nature of the remediation at given levels should differ. Research should be directed at determining which remedial methods are best at these different age levels, and also the effects of certain remedial procedures at one age level on subsequent levels.

Psycholinguistic disabilities can be ameliorated, not cured. The instructional goal of remediation is to have the learning disabled child reach a basic level of competence in his disability area so that he can meet the minimal academic and social demands made upon him in school, at home, and during adulthood. It is important to recognize that at the present time it may not be possible to "cure" most children's psycholinguistic disabilities. That is to say, they cannot be trained to continually function like non-learning disabled children in their disability areas. For most learning disabled children, remediation, at best, may be successful in ameliorating their disabilities; i.e., lessening the severity and extent.

In any research on remediation, test scores and observable behaviors must be used to operationally define the basic level of competence that is the goal for remediation with a given child. Amelioration of a learning disability should be measured in terms of the change in the child's intraindividual differences, and not comparisons with other children's profiles (i.e., interindividual differences).

Psycholinguistic training is part of a total remedial and compensatory teaching program. The overall educational program for any learning disabled child should include an interrelated remedial and compensatory teaching approach (Minskoff and Minskoff, 1974). Remedial teaching is necessary to have the child reach a basic level of competence in his disability area. Since psycholinguistic disabilities are not usually cured, but rather ameliorated, compensatory teaching is necessary to aid a child in mastering social and academic learnings by circumventing his disabilities and using his abilities. Any research on psycholinguistic training must recognize that such training alone is inadequate for providing a total education for the learning disabled, but rather, only one integral aspect.

Variables in Research on Remediation of Psycholinguistic Disabilities

There are three major factors to be described and controlled when conducting research on the question: *What types of remedial methods are most effective with what kinds of learning disabled children under what conditions?* These involve: the nature of the subjects, the treatment, and the experimental design. These variables must be considered when conducting research on published programs, such as the MWM Program, as well as unpublished teaching methods and materials. The following discussion is based on Minskoff's (1973) article, "Creating and Evaluating Remediation for the Learning Disabled."

Nature of the Subjects

1. *Learning disabled vs. non-learning disabled subjects.* Although it should go without saying that only learning disabled subjects should be used to investigate the efficacy of remediation of psycholinguistic disabilities, this has not been done in much of the past research.

2. *Nature of the learning disability.* Because of the heterogeneity of the learning disabled population, it is imperative that the disabilities of the subjects in any study be operationally defined so that the following questions can be answered. Of what population in the field of learning disabilities is this sample representative? Are the remedial methods under investigation effective for this particular population?

Such an operational definition must include explicit criteria for judging a child as having a psycholinguistic disability. Such a decision must be made by analyzing each subject's intraindividual differences. It is necessary to obtain an expected level of performance for a particular child in terms of ITPA scaled scores and language ages as well as specific academic and social behaviors. Then this subject's actual test scores and observed behaviors must be compared with his expected levels. The final diagnosis should reveal the general psycholinguistic disability area, specific subareas or symptoms, and level of functioning. Obviously, such a diagnosis must incorporate data from tests (especially the ITPA), diagnostic teaching, and systematic observation.

The final diagnosis must include indications of the severity and possible cause of each subject's disabilities. Although the cause of a disability cannot always be determined, it is imperative that a case history be made to determine the constitutional or environmental factors that may be associated with a subject's disability.

3. *Background characteristics.* It is necessary to analyze the background characteristics of age, learning abilities, IQ, social class, and race.

Subjects should not be pooled across age levels because children of various ages have different types of disabilities and need different types of treatment.

Subjects should be homogeneous with respect to areas of learning abilities so that all subjects can use the same areas as aids in remediation. These abilities can be identified from a comprehensive diagnosis of each subject's learning characteristics.

Only subjects at the same general level of intellectual functioning should be used. Since most of the learning disabled served in the schools are of average intelligence, it is important to use subjects with average or "potentially average" intelligence. If subjects with IQ scores in the retarded range who seem to have the "potential" for average intellectual functioning are used, the observable basis for making such an inference must be made explicit.

Finally, groups of subjects should be as similar as possible on social class and racial factors.

Nature of the Treatment

It is imperative that the treatment given be fully described so that the following fifteen criteria can be used to evaluate the remediation.

1. *Is the remediation directed at the subjects' psycholinguistic disabilities?* It should be obvious that a general approach in which the subjects' specific psycholinguistic disabilities are neither diagnosed nor treated cannot be defined as remediation.

Even when an individualized treatment approach is used, it is advisable that each study focus on evaluating remediation for one or, at the most, a few psycholinguistic areas. Designs in which there is treatment given for all twelve psycholinguistic areas are usually too complex and costly, especially since many efficacy studies are doctoral dissertations.

It studies are devoted to evaluating remediation for a single psycholinguistic area, then it is possible to fully describe both the nature of the subjects and the treatment. For example, a study might investigate the following hypothesis: "The asking of convergent, divergent, and evaluative thinking questions by teachers increases the subjects' Auditory Association scores on the ITPA and the number of such statements subjects give in their classroom performance." The subjects' pre- and post-treatment Auditory Association scores and their pre- and post-treatment statements in these categories can then be analyzed. In addition, the nature of the treatment can be fully described by analyzing the teacher's verbal interactions.

It should then be possible to compare the results of studies using different remedial techniques for the same psycholinguistic area, and eventually arrive at answers to questions such as, "How can Auditory Association best be trained?"

2. *Does the remediation fit the specific behavioral symptoms of the subjects?* In any remediation study there must be an analysis of the subareas of the psycholinguistic area given treatment. Once such an analysis is made, it is necessary to identify social and academic behaviors in each subarea which the subjects have not mastered. Then remediation is directed at training the subjects to master these social and academic behaviors.

3. *Is remediation at the subjects' level of functioning?* Remediation must not be given at the CA or MA level of the subjects, but must be at their current level of functioning in their disability subareas. Although the level of functioning may be couched in age scores, it is necessary to identify the discrete behaviors the subjects have and have not mastered.

4. *Do the subjects have learning abilities in the psycholinguistic areas used as aids for remediation?* First it is necessary to analyze the remedial methods being investigated to identify the areas that are to be used as aids. Then the diagnostic data for each subject must be analyzed to determine if each has the required abilities in these areas.

5. *Are both testing and teaching included in the remediation?* Both testing and teaching are inherent components of remediation which serve complementary purposes. Testing here does not involve formal tests; rather, it involves the clinical use of teaching

activities to continuously determine what a child has learned and what he has not learned. Naturally, testing is necessary before teaching to discover what learnings the subjects have not mastered so they can be taught. Testing is necessary after teaching to ascertain the degree to which the subjects have mastered the material that was presented.

In teaching, strategies are used to build in the desired responses if they have not been acquired, or to strengthen them if they have not been fully mastered.

Strategies differ for each remedial method and must be fully described. Unfortunately, many published remediation programs give descriptions of how to test, but not how to use specific strategies for instructional purposes.

6. *Is there a graduated sequence of learning in the remediation?* It is necessary to formulate a total learning sequence from the subjects' starting point to the final performance goals for the subjects. Then it is necessary to break this sequence of learning into small graduated steps. It then is possible to move subjects to higher levels of performance in their disability areas by providing remediation in these small steps.

7. *Is remediation directed at each subject's individual rate of progress?* Movement to a more difficult level of instruction in remediation must be geared to each subject's rate of progress, and not the group's readiness or a predetermined period of time.

Therefore, it is necessary to keep records of each subject's progress so it can be determined when he is ready to move to a more difficult level. To do this, it is necessary to establish a criterion level of mastery; i.e., the number of correct responses required to define a child's mastery of a particular learning.

8. *Is the content of the remediation of academic or social value to the subjects?* Most learning disabled children have much information and many skills to acquire because their disabilities have often prevented them from gaining these through traditional school instruction. Therefore, as many of these skills and facts must be provided through the content of the remediation. In addition, the problem of transfer is facilitated by making the content relevant to the current demands on the subjects.

9. *Is transfer built into the remediation?* A frequent complaint voiced about remediation is that there is no transfer from the remediation to the classroom or home setting. There must be guided opportunities for the subjects to apply learnings from the remedial setting to other situations.

10. *Is adequate time provided for the remediation?* Children with learning disabilities should not be expected to master tasks that they have not been able to master previously with traditional teaching in weeks, and possibly even months. To be effective, remediation for some subjects may have to be given over years. In addition, data on the length and frequency of the remediation must be stated because short frequent remedial sessions may be more effective than long, infrequent sessions.

11. *Was an adequate quantity of remediation provided?* There must be a quantitative description of the remedial content provided. For training of auditory and verbal disabilities, this may include a quantitative analysis of the different types of questions asked by the teacher; or for the training of visual areas, this might include the number of different types of worksheets provided.

12. *Are there restructuring strategies provided when subjects cannot master the remedial methods?* Many learning disabled children do not automatically master the remedial tasks as presented; therefore, all remedial methods must have reteaching strategies built in so that the probability of having a child master the learnings by different approaches can be increased.

13. *Can the remediation be given to an individual, small group, or large group?* The nature of the group given the remediation must be delineated so that it can be determined if the same method can be used with other types of groups.

14. *Is the teacher implementing the remedial methods as they are supposed to be?* It is necessary to obtain observational, tape-recorded, or videotaped data on the teachers providing the remediation to determine if they are, indeed, using the remediation as it is to be given.

15. *What training and experiental factors are necessary for a teacher to implement the remediation?* Studies on remediation must indicate the types of training necessary for the teacher to use the remediation as well as any required experiences with learning disabled children. Inferences can then be made with respect to the ability of teachers with different training and experience to use these remedial methods.

Experimental Design

There are two basic designs which can be used to evaluate the efficacy of remedial methods for psycholinguistic disabilities; one is a group design and the other is an individual design.

Group design.   Studies in which groups of subjects are used must begin with the evaluation of a large number of potential subjects to determine those who are most homogeneous. Each child's learning disabilities and abilities must be identified through testing, diagnostic teaching, and observation. Then those who are most homogeneous in terms of their disabilities and their background characteristics should be selected as subjects. Sets of three subjects should then be matched on the nature of their disabilities and background characteristics. Each of the three subjects in a set should be randomly placed in one of three treatment groups: experimental treatment, attention, and control. An attention group is necessary to rule out the effects of special attention as an explanation for any improvement of the experimental treatment subjects. The characteristics of the subjects in each of these three groups must be fully described so that it can be determined if they were well matched.

The treatment given to the experimental group must be described on the basis of the above fifteen criteria. In addition, it is necessary to analyze the treatment to determine if there was any teaching directly for the test used in the evaluation. It is also important to describe what was given to the attention group.

After treatment, the three groups of subjects should be reevaluated with the same measures as were used for diagnosis; i.e., tests, diagnostic teaching, and observations. The persons administering and scoring the evaluative data must not know the group placement of each subject.

It is necessary to project for each subject the goal performance, after remediation, in terms of specific test scores and observed academic and social behaviors in remedial, classroom, and out-of-school settings. Then the post-treatment test and behavioral results for each subject should be compared to these proposed performance goals. It is imperative that an individual analysis be made of each subject's progress. Analysis of only group data results in the loss of precious information. Obviously, the role of traditionally used statistics is somewhat limited in making such an analysis. Finally, the conclusions generated from such studies should rarely be total acceptance or rejection, but rather qualified conclusions regarding the effectiveness of the remediation as given in the study with the type of subjects used.

Individual design.   An N=1 case study design can be a sound approach if comprehensive subject and treatment data are given. As Newcomer and Hammill indicate, there is a problem associated with this design in that psycholinguistic areas usually improve with age. However, this problem can be minimized if adequate baseline data are provided to show that the subject had not mastered learnings in his psycholinguistic disability area over a number of previous years with traditional instruction. Improvement after treatment can then be attributed to the introduction of the remedial method.

PAST, PRESENT, AND FUTURE DIRECTIONS OF RESEARCH ON REMEDIATION OF PSYCHOLINGUISTIC DISABILITIES

To place in perspective the research that has been conducted on the efficacy of remediation of psycholinguistic disabilities heretofore, it is necessary to understand the current status of the field of learning disabilities.

The state of the field can be grasped by applying the historical periods Caldwell proposed for the development of Head Start programs (1974). The first period was that of optimism. The ITPA was devised and became widely used. Large numbers of children were labeled as learning disabled, and their problems seemed to become instantly comprehensible and amenable to treatment. Underlying this period was the covert promise of cures for all types of problems in all kinds of children. To paraphrase the Emma Lazarus poem on the Statue of Liberty, special education said to general education: "Give me your underachievers, your problems, your children yearning to learn as only we can teach."

The second period of skepticism entered as the results of efficacy studies began to indicate that many remedial methods may not have been effective with various types of children. This skepticism, which is voiced by Newcomer and Hammill in this review, is healthy and, hopefully, will continue if there is ever to be a solid foundation for remedial treatment.

The third period of disillusionment is where many in the field of learning disabilities are at the present time. These periods of optimism, skepticism, and disillusionment may be reflected in Newcomer and Hammill's findings that 52 percent of the efficacy studies from 1962–66 showed positive results, 31 percent from 1967–69, and 21 percent from 1970–73.

However, there is a lethal danger associated with this period of disillusionment because it can lead to the abolition of treatment programs for children with psycholinguistic disabilities. A comparable situation existed in the field of mental retardation when efficacy studies on special classes for the educable mentally retarded indicated limited success (e.g., Goldstein et al., 1965). In this period of disillusionment, the field of mental retardation eliminated special classes and mainstreamed great numbers of the retarded. Currently, there are many retarded children floundering in regular programs and not receiving the special social learning curriculum and teaching methods they need. Hopefully, the field of learning disabilities will not respond to the findings of efficacy studies by eliminating psycholinguistic training programs for the learning disabled.

It is hoped that Newcomer and Hammill's review will provide the impetus for the entry into the fourth period, that of consolidation. In this period there should be a healthy skepticism which is the basis for conducting improved research on the efficacy of remedial methods for psycholinguistic disabilities; and then, the utilization of this research as the foundation for providing "tested" remediation in the schools.

Reaction to Dr. Minskoff's Viewpoint

Dr. Esther Minskoff's discussion focuses on the issue of the efficacy of psycholinguistic training from a research perspective. She perceives the analysis of the literature which was presented, particularly in chapter 4, as being overly simplistic since it attempts to answer the question "Is psycholinguistic training effective?" She believes a more appropriate question would be: "What types of remedial methods are most effective with what kinds of learning disabled children under what conditions?" She notes that studies which utilize dissimilar subjects, treatments, and training periods are not comparable. In support of her opinion she critiques the efficacy studies included in our review, offers her conceptualization of the assumptions which should underlie efficacy studies and discusses past, present, and future directions in the field of psycholinguistic training.

In discussing the inadequacies within the existent literature, Dr. Minskoff specifically elaborates on the fact that the experimental subjects, for the most part, were not "learning disabled" in accordance with the United States Office of Education 1969 definition, implying that the efficacy of psycholinguistic training must be tested on that population alone. Consequently she disregards or at least minimizes the results of studies which used psycholinguistic activities for developmental purposes, such as supplements to reading and/or readiness instruction, or which employed non-learning disabled children, such as "mentally retarded" or "cultural disadvantaged" children as subjects. She also disputes conclusions gained from research on "learning disabled" children which failed to establish stringent criteria for subject uniformity such as communality in their types of learning disabilities, as well as similarity in the etiology of their conditions and their background characteristics.

It is true that the studies included in our review involved diverse subjects, i.e., mental retardates, underachieving and/or culturally different children, as well as the learning disabled children. Our justification is that the literature reflects the actual situation in the public schools relevant to psycholinguistic training. Many children, essentially underachievers, are designated as learning disabled, despite varied cultural, socioeconomic, and etiological factors. They are diagnosed, usually with the ITPA, and receive various types of psycholinguistic training. In addition, mentally retarded children with language problems are the frequent recipients of efforts to improve their underlying psycholinguistic deficits. In short, educators are apparently convinced that psycholinguistic training programs are useful in mitigating a multitude of problems which school children experience.

Seemingly there is a good reason why educators hold this belief. Most of the authors of psycholinguistic training programs expressly state that their materials are for use with all kinds of children who do poorly in school and do not limit their programs for exclusive use with "learning disabled" children. In fact, Dr. Minskoff, along with her coauthors of the *Program for Developing Language Abilities*, state that their materials are appropriate for developmental use and certainly mention no restrictions as to types of children for whom the program is suitable. They state that:

> A secondary purpose of the MWM program is for developmental teaching of language to children aged 3 to 7 who are not learning disabled. The MWM Program is appropriate for such children because it includes systematic teaching activities arranged in a carefully graduated sequence of learning (p. 1) . . . Any nursery school, kindergarten, first grade teacher, or teacher of a special class for the mentally retarded can use the MWM Program developmentally. In addition teachers of extended readiness or transitional classes can use the program to build-in necessary language skills in their students (p. 13).

In light of this we do not understand Dr. Minskoff's objections to efficacy studies relating to developmental training programs, since the researchers have merely followed the directions suggested by the program authors. Seemingly these studies reflect the general state of the art in psycholinguistic training and their attempts to investigate the relative success or failure of training under diverse conditions is valid. If the efficacy of psycholinguistic training can only be determined on severe cases of learning disability which evidence psycholinguistic deficits, it seems equally logical for authors of such programs to avoid overgeneralizing the applicability of their materials to populations other than "remedial" cases.

Dr. Minskoff's second objection related to the inconsistencies in the nature of psycholinguistic treatments. Specifically she notes that (1) developmental programs were used often in a generalized approach (where all children received the same activities), (2) individual learning disabilities were not directly related to instruction, and (3) instructional time and teacher competence varied. Although neither information regarding teacher competency nor specific psycholinguistic profiles for each subject were mentioned in the studies received, variables such as hours and duration of training; age, type, and number of subjects; and type of training program were noted by the researchers and the reader may inspect table 12 for each study of interest. In addition, table 13 divides the literature on eight important dimensions so that the reader has some appreciation of the value of psycholinguistic training under those conditions. In our opinion it is unrealistic to expect independent studies to have identical designs so that they might be matched on all possible dimensions. It seems appropriate to conclude that if a program is advocated for broad application in the schools, it is fair to evaluate the efficacy of the research on the common dimensions which are identifiable. The overview which we present demonstrates the "general" results of their training programs.

Dr. Minskoff's third objection to the research related to the methodological weaknesses in the experimental design. We grant this point but are compelled to add that it is the only research available and therefore must be reported despite its imperfections. We might note, for the sake of argument, that Minskoff's assumption that the methodological weaknesses of the research made it difficult to obtain significant results in favor of the experimental programs is disputable. It seems plausible, at least to us, that if the sources of error in these studies were corrected, the results would be even more bleak regarding the merits of psycholinguistic training than they are. Several of the errors in design include instances where (1) the teacher-pupil ratio differed between treatment groups resulting in the experimental pupils receiving more individualized attention than their "matched" controls; (2) individuals who were already committed to,

and possibly prejudiced in favor of, the experimental program provided the training; (3) Hawthorne or novelty effect was not adequately controlled for; (4) it was concluded that the experimental
subjects had outperformed their control group when in fact the difference between them was due to the regression of the control subjects rather than to the improvement of the trained subjects, and so
forth. It is also interesting to note that advocates of psycholinguistic
training (to our knowledge Esther Minskoff is not one) are not so
critical of the quality of existing research when the results are generally supportive of their positions. For example, studies by Wiseman
(1965), Hart (1963), and Smith (1962) are referred to by Kirk and Kirk
(1971), by McLeod in his paper which follows, and by others as showing the beneficial effects of ITPA-related remediation on learning defects. Upon close examination of Wiseman's study, an interesting
pilot effort using mentally retarded children as subjects, it was found
that only ten youngsters were involved—a fact which should make
one circumspect in generalizing its results. In addition to employing
small numbers of retarded and cerebral palsied subjects, neither Hart
nor Smith made statistical comparisons of the differences between
the performance of their experimental and control subjects on the
ITPA subtests. Although these efforts may be interpreted as credible,
early attempts to accrue information regarding psycholinguistic learning patterns in children, they can hardly be regarded as exemplary
demonstrations of tight, well designed research. Neither can their
results be readily accepted as evidence of the benefits of psycholinguistic training, especially when compared to the steady accumulation of negative findings based on research which used basically the
same designs but which had been strengthened by the use of larger
samples, longer training periods, and adequate statistical analyses.

In the next section of her discussion, Minskoff provides guidelines
for designing and implementing research on the efficacy of remediating psycholinguistic disabilities. She offers seven underlying assumptions which she apparently accepts as "truths." Since we have reason
to doubt the validity of certain of these assumptions, it is useful to
discuss them in detail.

The assumptions are as follows: (1) the learning disabled children
represent a heterogeneous population, (2) psycholinguistic disabilities can be identified, (3) psycholinguistic disabilities can be
trained, (4) psycholinguistic functioning is related to social and
academic learning, (5) psycholinguistic training differs at various age
levels, (6) psycholinguistic disabilities can be ameliorated, not cured,
and (7) psycholinguistic training is part of a total remedial and compensatory teaching program.

The first point which refers to the heterogeneity of learning disabled children is a given and need not be pursued further. The second assumption, however, that psycholinguistic disabilities can be identified, warrants extensive exploration. In her discussion of the diagnosability of psycholinguistic disabilities, Dr. Minskoff apparently regards the ITPA as necessary but not sufficient for the task. She recommends further fragmenting of ITPA subareas to increase the number of tasks measuring each construct. In so doing she demonstrates her belief that the constructs included in the twelve ITPA subtests represent the main dimensions of psycholinguistic development. In reality these areas lack ready acceptance as important psycholinguistic dimensions among most modern psycholinguists; they simply represent Samuel Kirk's attempts to operationalize the Osgood model of language behavior. Those who would utilize an alternate model for psycholinguistic development might develop a totally varied approach to assessment, i.e., one which measures syntax, semantics, or other aspects of language through expression and understanding of English phrases and sentences.

Additionally, we have indicated elsewhere in this book that the construct validity of certain ITPA subtests, as well as the predictive and diagnostic validity of the ITPA in relationship to academic achievement, is in doubt. Consequently, it does not seem appropriate to utilize these constructs as models for developing further psycholinguistic diagnostic tasks. For example, if the Visual Sequential Memory subtest cannot be proven to actually measure the psychological construct "visual sequential memory" as it is defined in the Kirk-Osgood theory, it is certainly inappropriate to use it to diagnose a child's deficit in that area. Furthermore, if discrete measurement of the task which is labeled "visual sequential memory" does not appear to relate to children's academic progress, the importance of developing additional submeasures of this construct is questionable. Even if we assume that Minskoff, Wiseman, and Minskoff have developed superior tasks to tap this construct, we must insist that since these are selected arbitrarily, they must be shown to have construct, predictive, and diagnostic validity through empirical study. In other words, they must be subjected to the same extensive validity and reliability investigations as were the original twelve ITPA subtests. Without this sort of substantiation, these subtasks might seem sound intuitively to their creators, but they have no proven value for diagnosis of psycholinguistic disabilities.

Minskoff's third assumption is that psycholinguistic processes can be trained. The validity of that assumption is what chapter 4 is about. Unfortunately, the evidence gathered thus far is not encouraging. At best Dr. Minskoff is justified in stating that the current results, while generally unfavorable, are not conclusive and that further research of improved design must be undertaken. Relevant to that issue we are distressed by the fact that the authors of training programs have failed, for the most part, to provide well-designed validity research prior to making their materials available for use with children. Although a dearth of such research on program validation is a common state of affairs in education, it often results in the unfortunate misuse of programs.

We agree with Dr. Minskoff when she refers to the importance of making tools available to teachers so that they might not be discouraged from working with learning disabled children. On the other hand, we appreciate the necessity for setting realistic expectations for the use of such tools and of discouraging program application when it is not beneficial to children. This concern brings us to Dr. Minskoff's fourth assumption, i.e., that psycholinguistic functioning is related to social and academic learning. Since Dr. Minskoff is referring to the ITPA, the evidence regarding that test's lack of predictive and concurrent validity relevant to academics must be brought to bear on that point (see chapter 3). Her charge that the primarily unsupportive research in this area is marred by errors of oversimplification is difficult for us to understand. Apparently she regards it as oversimplistic to use ITPA subtests exclusively to test the relationship of ITPA constructs with achievement, reiterating that subskills in these areas must be developed and related to achievement. Quite naturally, the research available which was designed to validate the ITPA constructs dealt with the content of that test. By and large these variables failed to relate significantly to reading, spelling, and arithmetic as measured by a variety of assessment devices. At present, there is little reason to assume that the MWM's, or other program's, conception of skills in these areas will correlate with achievement either. Based on the existent evidence, perhaps it is somewhat rash for psycholinguistic trainers to suggest to educators that their programs will improve academic achievement, a premise which has little basis in fact. A more judicious attainment for program developers might relate to demonstrating that improvement in psycholinguistic skills results from psycholinguistic training.

We note that in her discussion of the relationships between psycholinguistics and academic achievement Dr. Minskoff advocates school-related activities to train psycholinguistic functions. For example, she recommends training visual sequential memory deficits with sequences of letters which she hypothesizes will relate to reading by the visual method. If the ultimate goal is to teach reading, teaching sequences of letters to train memory processes in the hope that this improved mental function will eventually result in improved reading skill is far less efficient than simply teaching sequences of letters called words in order to build a basic sight vocabulary for reading.

We also must admit to doubts regarding the direct usefulness of psycholinguistic training for social learning. Although Dr. Minskoff speculates about the importance of the child's ability to understand inflectional differences (Auditory Reception) or to interpret body language (Visual Reception) as determinants of social interaction skill, the relationships appear remote to us. Her position on this topic seems to illustrate the types of general, intuitively based claims which are made for psycholinguistic training. It is small wonder that training programs in the schools are used extensively and often indiscriminately to fulfill rather vague goals.

We do not have cause to take serious issue with Dr. Minskoff's fifth, sixth, and seventh assumptions. Her fifth, the relationship of psycholinguistic abilities to age is obviously true, i.e., children's skills vary with their level of maturation. Her sixth point, that psycholinguistic disabilities can be ameliorated, not cured, is disturbing only in that it serves to illustrate a somewhat unfortunate acceptance of a medical frame of reference which equates poor achievement with disease and which is usually unwarranted when dealing with children's learning problems. However, this issue is not germane to our discussion and need not receive further elaboration here. Regarding her seventh point, that psycholinguistic training is part of a total remedial and compensatory teaching program and is not sufficient to provide a total education, we might note that in our opinion the question is not the necessity of compensatory instructional programs for educating certain children, but the value of the psycholinguistic training component.

In order to provide the reader with a synopsis of our position regarding the entire issue of psycholinguistic training, we will clearly state that while we agree with Dr. Minskoff's call for better designed and controlled research, we see no need to dismiss in total the results of the existent studies. We feel that the reported literature raises some important doubts regarding the efficacy of these programs and that the burden of demonstrating their value falls squarely on the shoulders of those individuals who advocate psycholinguistic training. At this point in time, the most supportive statement possible would be that psycholinguistic training programs are still in their formative, experimental stages and could not contain any ascertation regarding their demonstrated benefits to children.

A Reaction to
Psycholinguistics in the Schools

John McLeod

In clinical diagnosis courses, I have always impressed upon students the need to try to encapsulate their major findings and recommendations into the opening contact paragraph (a) so that the reader might be prepared for the thrust of the more detailed report which follows and (b) in case the overtaxed recipient does not read beyond the opening paragraph. It is a pity that the authors of the text under review did not adopt a similar tactic, by incorporating some of the excellent, overdue (at least in public in the U.S.), and insightful observations on training programs of the final chapter into the perceptive and promising preface. Unfortunately, between the preface and chapter 4 are three rather undistinguished chapters, which add little to the overall work. The first of these intervening chapters is entitled, somewhat grandiosely, "Application of Psycholinguistics to *Education*" (my italics) and fulfills its stated aim of providing a superficial grasp of psycholinguistics. Chapter 2, entitled "The Illinois Test of Psycholinguistic Abilities," combines descriptive facts, speculation, personal opinion, and inaccuracies related to the content and purpose of the ITPA, while chapter 3 arrives at conclusions related to the diagnostic validity of the ITPA, although the relevance to the conclusions of much of the chapter's content is not particularly obvious.

More specific comment on these three chapters will be made presently, but attention will first be focused on more basic and far-reaching issues raised or suggested by the preface and final chapter.

The preface states that the educator's approach to psycholinguistics is based on the assumptions that

a. psycholinguistic constructs are measurable by available tests;
b. measured psycholinguistic constructs are in some way directly [*sic*] related to school failure; and
c. identified psycholinguistic problems are remediable by *readily available programs* or techniques.

The validity of this penetrating analysis cannot be denied. In fact, the analysis probably does not go far enough. Two further assumptions on which much current practice is based are that diagnostic tests are competently administered and interpreted and that remediated psycholinguistic skills produce a positive, beneficial transfer effect to basic school subjects. As the ITPA is not the easiest test in the world to administer, the assumption of diagnostician competency—particularly in a context of graduate student research—is not one that can be sustained with confidence. The assumption of transferability to more "marketable" skills of any psycholinguistic improvements accruing from remediation is one with respect to which some of us (McLeod 1966, p. 198; Kirk and McLeod 1966, p. 182) have been counseling caution for some time.

Caution, or healthy skepticism, is the note on which Newcomer and Hammill's discussion ends. They rightly draw attention to the amount of time, money, and effort that is currently being spent on programs designed to increase psycholinguistic skills* when, for a variety of suggested reasons, the observed improvement in automatic level skills particularly has been less than exciting. (Incidentally, the suggestion that future research might throw light on inadequate research methodology raises intriguing speculation.) They conclude that allegedly remedial programs need to be viewed cautiously and monitored with care. This is an excellent sentiment and one that should be emblazoned over the entrance to the publishers' extravaganza of materials high on packaging but low on validation, which adorn the annual conferences of CEC (McLeod, 1970, p. 16).

However, a likely consequence of the skepticism which Newcomer and Hammill's book might well engender is not careful monitoring (and the evolutionary improvement of technique?) but rather on outright jettisoning of babies together with bathwater.

We live in a "bitty" age and culture when complex social issues are reduced—maybe for Mr. Gallup and/or the computer—to a simple "for" or "against" opinion. The phenomenon seems to have spilled over into Special Education where, for many people, salvation (or damnation, with nothing in between) is to be had through the intercession of Delacato, or Engelmann, or Frostig, or Gillingham or Kirk, a positive reaction to one automatically precluding sympathetic consideration of the others.

Charles Fries (1963) has criticized much of what passes for educational research as lacking the two fundamental characteristics of a

---

*The final section of the Newcomer and Hammill book, excellent though it is, relates—possibly inadvertently—to the improvement of psycholinguistic skills only, rather than to basic school achievement. Unless there is positive payoff, this reviewer would agree with Mann (e.g., 1967) that the effort is something of an exercise in futility.

science, namely, that it be cumulative and impersonal. Osgood (1957) assessed the significance of his theoretical model as one which might provide an "impetus for research, and which can give us at least the illusion of understanding." In turn, McCarthy and Kirk (1961) recognized Osgood's model as "being of great convenience, since (it) defined the type of tasks required" in diagnosing psycholinguistic functioning, because the assessment of language processes "of young handicapped children is . . . a necessary pre-requisite to planning appropriate educational or remedial pro-grams" (Kirk and Bateman, 1964). It was within this declared context of diagnosis of young educationally handicapped children in an ar-ticulated and cumulative developmental sequence of theoretical and applied research that the present writer approached the advent of the new experimental ITPA which made its appearance in the early 1960s. At the time of my first encounter with the original ITPA, I had just completed a research study which compared the WISC subtest scores of retarded readers with those of achieving children. The results were in line with the general findings of other re-searchers in this area, namely that Vocabulary, Arithmetic, Informa-tion, Coding and Digit Span discriminated over and above total IQ in favor of controls. What was somewhat puzzling was that despite their discriminating power, Coding and Digit Span did not correlate significantly with IQ for either the experimental group or the con-trols. The model on which the ITPA was based helped to make sense of the findings, for the two subtests were clearly tapping what we now refer to as Automatic level skills, whereas the IQ is predomi-nantly a Representational level assessment. In the disinterested un-derfunded climate of an Australian university-affiliated facility in 1964, where the word Kirk evoked association of a Scottish rather than an American institution, we carried out a critical "consumer analysis" of this new expensive, experimental American test. With thirty-four consecutive referrals of severely retarded readers, we found that psycholinguistic age correlated significantly better with reading age than did mental age, chronological age being partialled out in each case. Moreover, multiple regression showed that the automatic level subtests were the three best predictors of reading age in underachieving children (McLeod, 1965). In a subsequent, more rigorously controlled experiment with grade two children, the ITPA discriminated severely retarded readers from unselected con-trols at the .01 level after covarying for WISC Full Scale IQ, while the Grammatic Closure, Auditory Sequential Memory, and Auditory Re-ception subtests further discriminated between the groups after covarying for uncontaminated ITPA total psycholinguistic age (McLeod, 1965).

Other idiosyncratic and experimental research carried out in Brisbane at that time (McLeod, 1968; Hart, 1963) reinforced the belief that the ITPA constituted an advance on existing intelligence tests that were in general clinical use *within the context of providing relevant diagnostic information about young educationally retarded children*. It was recognized (Kirk and McLeod, 1966) that the ITPA "is not a final answer to all questions of disabilities in children," but rather that it "represents a beginning phase . . . in the development of the applied branch of the science of psycholinguistics." Subsequent experience, including Newcomer and Hammill's chapter 3 review of research which is mostly inappropriate and/or based on simplistic notions of diagnosis,* gives no cause to modify that original assessment.

Unfortunately, the ITPA became a boon for graduate students in search of a thesis or researchers in search of a project, by presenting a new multiscored vehicle that could be compared with established psycho-educational tests, or be used to survey the psycholinguistic profiles of an array of target populations from Canadian Indians to Australian aborigines. And, by yielding nine or ten subscores, it was a godsend for any researcher with access to a computer and a principal components program. In much of the reported research its intended purpose as a clinical diagnostic instrument was lost sight of.

Clinically, too, the ITPA has been inextricably linked with another bandwagon, that of Learning Disabilities. The term "learning disability" was introduced by Kirk with the laudable motive of circumventing what, from an educator's standpoint, was a red herring debate concerning the neurology of basic educational failure. Learning Disability has itself become a reified source of controversy, one byproduct being comprehensive analyses of tests and remedial techniques in terms of the dimensions of the Osgood model. The writer recently learned of a graduate study at a prestigious U.S. university which aimed to analyze the whole of the Revised Stanford-Binet test in terms of channel, level, and process. This fad, of analyzing every known educational process into psycholinguistic constructs precipitated the reaction of Task Analysis, resulting in yet another example of an "either-or" confrontation when the art of remediation calls for

---

*The simplistic nature of some diagnostic notions of the relation of psycholinguistic skill deficiency to learning disabilities and inappropriateness of many correlational studies will be treated in greater detail later.

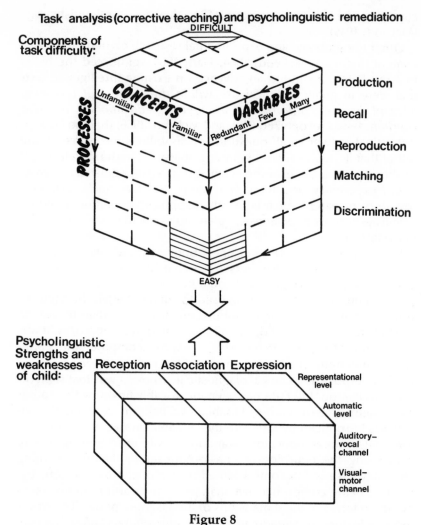

Figure 8

Task Analysis (corrective teaching) and Psycholinguistic Remediation

a merging, integration, or balance between task analysis, which breaks down presenting symptoms into more elementary tasks with an upward synthesis from basic psycholinguistic strengths and weaknesses. This diagnostic strategy is illustrated in figures 8 and 9.

Chapter 1, which might have been more appropriately titled "Psycholinguistics and Exceptional Children" or "Psycholinguistics and Learning Disability," provides a fairly extensive, but admittedly superficial, discussion of Chomsky's work and current theories of

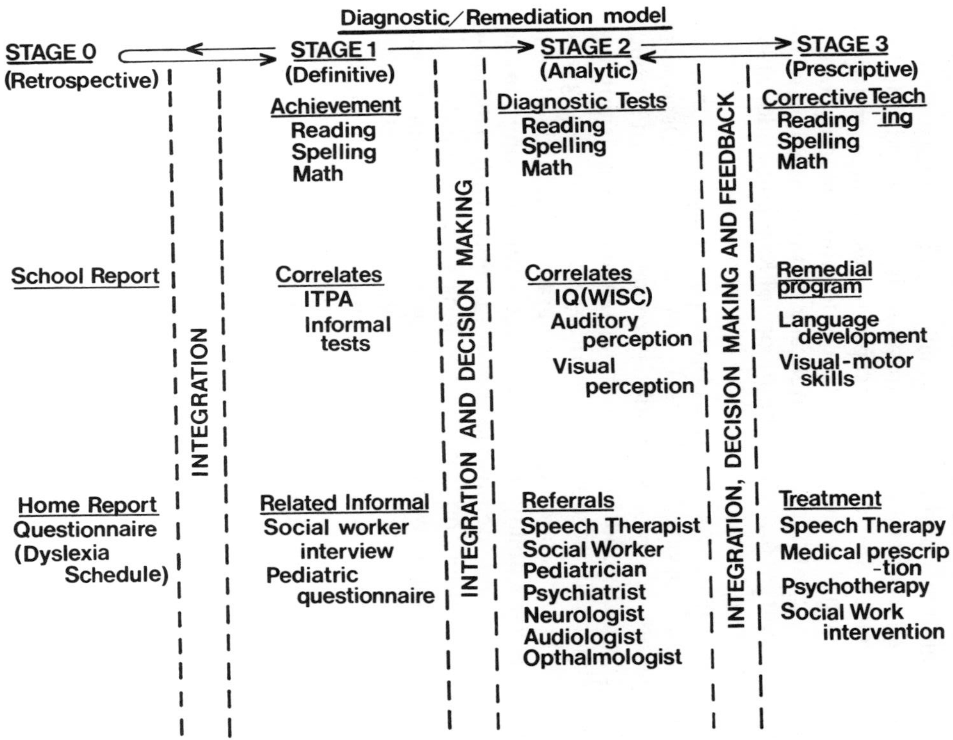

Diagnostic/Remediation model

STAGE 0 → STAGE 1 → STAGE 2 → INTEGRATION, DECISION MAKING AND FEEDBACK → STAGE 3
(Retrospective)   (Definitive)   (Analytic)   (Prescriptive)

STAGE 0 (Retrospective)

School Report

Home Report
Questionnaire
(Dyslexia
    Schedule)

INTEGRATION

STAGE 1 (Definitive)

Achievement
Reading
Spelling
Math

Correlates
ITPA
Informal
tests

Related Informal
Social worker
interview
Pediatric
questionnaire

INTEGRATION AND DECISION MAKING

STAGE 2 (Analytic)

Diagnostic Tests
Reading
Spelling
Math

Correlates
IQ(WISC)
Auditory
perception
Visual
perception

Referrals
Speech Therapist
Social Worker
Pediatrician
Psychiatrist
Neurologist
Audiologist
Opthalmologist

INTEGRATION, DECISION MAKING AND FEEDBACK

STAGE 3 (Prescriptive)

Corrective Teach-ing
Reading
Spelling
Math

Remedial
program
Language
development
Visual-motor
skills

Treatment
Speech Therapy
Medical prescrip-tion
Psychotherapy
Social Work
intervention

Figure 9

Diagnostic/Remediation Model

133

psycholinguistics. * The reference to Chomsky's 1957 work *Syntactic Structures* to the exclusion of his 1965 *Aspects of the Theory of Syntax* and to some extent his 1966 *Topics in the Theory of Generative Grammar* overlooks the ontogenetic development of the linguist's theory of grammar and its influence on psychologists. Very briefly, the 1957 Chomsky deals with kernel sentences and transformational grammar and only marginally with phonology. The traditional separation of grammar and meaning is maintained. The 1965 Chomsky develops the earlier concepts in his surface and deep structure and, what is more important, adds the semantic component. It may be mentioned parenthetically that the inclusion of the semantic element incorporates the theory of Katz and Fodor (1963) that Newcomer and Hammill allude to in a cursory way.

Arising from the above, it should also be pointed out that the view that Chomskyian psycholinguistics is "in" while the Osgoodian three-stage mediation model is "out" is premature. It is not so much that Skinner or Osgood is wrong about language acquisition and that Chomsky is right; rather, they see different aspects of language. Osgood (1971) points out that generative grammar is inadequate to explain a speaker's ability to use language without taking into account perceptual and cognitive factors in addition to linguistic ones. Moreover, Newcomer and Hammill overlook some recent theoretical and experimental work on language behavior from Kansas (McLean, Yoder, and Schiefelbusch, 1972; Schiefelbusch, 1972). These authors demonstrate that developmental psycholinguistics provides the framework for language development of exceptional children while operant conditioning provides the techniques for language habilitation.

While the factor analytic studies conducted by the authors and their colleagues (Newcomer et al., 1974; Hare et al., 1973) have merit, some questions arise:

a. The finding of lack of modality clustering is at variance with some sound analyses (Meyers, 1969; Leong, 1974).
b. The suggestion of validating the ITPA subtests with such as tests by Lee, Carrow, Berko (p. 39) is circular, as the ITPA and these tests are based on different psycholinguistic premises (as the authors point out) and hence are expected to tap

---

*The writer is indebted to Dr. C. K. Leong for suggestions incorporated in this section of the review.

slightly different domains. Any attempt to factor analyze the ITPA with these other tests will produce discordant results.

c. Review of literature on the factor analytic aspects is less than adequate (e.g., the chapter in Lester Mann's *First Review of Special Education* on the constructs of the ITPA and the ingenious and sophisticated analysis of Doughtie et al. (1974) might have been mentioned.)

Chapter 2 attempts to present an overview of the rationale, content, reliability, and validity of the ITPA. We are again told (without any reference) that "Osgood's theory of language is no longer considered plausible by most modern psycholinguists," and that "many individuals" feel that the ITPA is based on an inadequate or incorrect conceptualization of language development. With hindsight, perhaps it would have been preferable if the ITPA had been originally associated with Wepman's (1964) clinical model rather than Osgood's behavioral model. The Wepman model, which is essentially identical with that of Osgood, has the virtue of having been developed in a clinical context and therefore has a visibly closer affinity with the purpose of the ITPA. We might have been spared some of the more ridiculous assertions of some factor analysts who have effectively equated cheese and chalk* by declaring, for instance, that visual reception and verbal expression are measuring the same general language factor.

The section which describes the actual subtests of the ITPA suggests that the authors are less intimately acquainted with the test than might be expected from someone engaged in a critical analysis. For example, although several of their illustrative items do actually appear in the test (so that, presumably, there is no deliberate attempt to camouflage actual test content) three "examples" are nowhere to be found in the test. (e.g., "Do ponies fly?" "Show me what you do with this" in the manual expression, and the "cheese" example of Visual Association.) Interpretation of a weakness in Auditory Memory and Auditory Reception as resembling the profile of a child with a hearing deficit (p. 32) is a rather extraordinary clinical observation; perhaps in the reference to this observation as a "premise" rather than a deduction there is more validity than the authors had intended.

---

*Presumably, an analytical chemist might consider that cheese and chalk are two aspects of the same substance, being made of calcium, carbon, and oxygen.

It is somewhat surprising to find Newcomer and Hammill to be more sanguine than Kirk and Paraskevopoulos about the test's reliability,* for the reliabilities of some subtests are lower than one had hoped. While the reliability of the ITPA subtests, and total test score, generally compare with those of a test such as the WISC, one fact which is perhaps insufficiently stressed or appreciated is that the ITPA needs to have greater reliability than an IQ test because of the way in which the test is (or should be) used. In the case of a test such as the WISC, it is usually the Verbal Performance and/or Full Scale IQ that is of clinical interest rather than individual subtest scores. The total WISC test score is sufficiently robust to be able to tolerate an unreliable subtest or two, whether the unreliability is inherent in the test, the result of inept administration, or arises from variability in children's performance. With the ITPA, on the other hand, the total psycholinguistic age is of only relatively inci-dental interest in a clinical situation. It is the comparison of indi-vidual subtest scores which influences diagnosis and prescriptive programming, so that the inevitably more modest reliability of differences between subtest scores can lead to inappropriate inter-pretations. Regrettably, the authors' observation that a child's test performance can result in a lengthy instructional prescription is probably true and, if so, reflects the teacher's inadequate prepara-tion. Diagnostic information derived from the ITPA (or any other test) should be used to structure remedial strategy and procedure for short-term goals, which must be confirmed, extended, or modified in the light of diagnostic teaching experience by means of some sort of feedback loop (Cartwright, 1972). Hence the two-way arrows be-tween stages 2 and 3 in figure 8.

The factor analysis of Newcomer et al. (1974) is a commendable attempt to analyze the ITPA in a more meaningful way than most previous analyses, although it is unfortunate that the sample (age range 105 to 118 months; average intelligence range) must have contained children who were at or above the effective ceiling for the test. There is an example of a certain dogmatism which surfaces from time to time when the authors assert that, apart from the Visual Closure subtest, "the visual channel is completely without substan-tiation as a valid dimension." Clinical experience suggests that this

---

*The matter of reliability is quite important to their subsequent arguments. By accepting the subtests as adequately reliable, they conclude that the model is in-valid. Inconclusive research findings might, alternatively, be accounted for by unreliable measurement of valid concepts.

statement is demonstrably absurd, but there are also other factorial studies (McLeod, 1966b; Leong, 1974; Doughtie et al., 1974) which have provided contradictory results. Perhaps the apparent confusion stems from the fact that as Thurstone (1948) found, a perceptual factor may transcend sensory modalities, a position consistent with an analysis of the ITPA carried out by McLeod (1966b).

The survey of diagnostic validity studies also does less than justice to the consistent detection of deficient automatic level skills of educationally disabled children (Bateman, 1964).

It is difficult to know where to begin in responding to chapter 3. Reference will be made later to some specific points, but initially, remarks will be confined to four more fundamental issues which have implications for much of the content of this chapter:

1. the clinical relationship between presenting symptoms and possibly causal factors;
2. the appropriateness of correlational studies;
3. the validity of head counts;
4. the effect of intelligence.

The Relationship between Presenting Symptoms and
Possible Causal Factors

Since educationists discovered the product-moment correlation coefficient, it seems to have generally been tacitly assumed that what might be a cause-and-effect relationship must be expressed in terms of a first- or second-order correlation between two continuous variables. This view is oversimplistic. For example, a highly significant relationship between measured intelligence and reading would be found if the scores of ten-year-old children were compared. But there would be virtually zero correlation between the measured intelligence and reading scores of two-year-old children, because in other words, there is a threshold, below which correlation is insignificant and above which it is highly significant. Likewise, if a modest threshold of (say) sound blending or phonemic discriminating ability is necessary in order to read the printed word, development beyond which is superfluous, then a situation as illustrated in figure 10 would apply.

In the simplified diagram, the correlation between reading and the psycholinguistic variable is zero, for children scoring above the critical threshold on the psycholinguistic variable. Below the threshold, there is a positive correlation. The shaded area represents children who are failing in reading for other causes. An overall

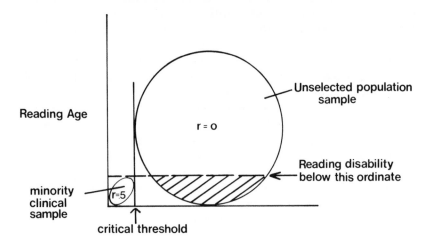

Psycholinguistic Skill Age

Figure 10

*Correlation and Clinical Relationship between
Presenting Symptom and Associated Factors*

correlational study of the total population fails to penetrate the reality of such a situation.

Again, the inclination to look for a simple one-to-one relationship between "cause" and effect leads us to assume that a "cause" is both necessary and sufficient, whereas it might be necessary but not sufficient in itself. As an illustration, it will be recalled that from his earlier work, Bowlby (1956) suggested that early hospitalization of infants produced emotional scars for life when, in fact, many children survive early hospitalization without obvious disastrous effects. One explanation, taking into account work by Money (1969), Pasamanick and Knobloch (1961), and Zangwill (1960), might be in terms of the 2 x 2 classification illustrated in figure 11. The two vertical columns might classify children according to whether they are what Zangwill would call cerebral ambilaterals or, if you like, children with latent brain dysfunction, and in the second column children with cerebral dominance or, to use a naive term, what we might call intact brains. And the two horizontal rows could classify children as, in the first row, those with traumatic experience in infancy and in the second row, those with maternal security in infancy. Children in the second column, that is children with what we might call "intact brains," are O. K. whether or not they have a traumatic experience, and similarly children in the second row are unlikely to have problems because they have maternal security. Therefore children in the pigeon-holes b, c, and d are not liable to have problems but the children in pigeon-hole a, i.e., the children with latent brain dysfunction and who have a traumatic experience in infancy, these are the children that we might consider to be at risk.

Applying an analogous argument to the case of the child with a learning disability, the detection of a deficient psycholinguistic skill provides information about what might well be a necessary contributing factor but not always a sufficient factor in itself. All this has intriguing implications for clinical analysis but is depressing as far as correlation coefficients are concerned.

The Appropriateness of Correlation Studies

The ITPA was developed as a "practical clinical procedure for the diagnosis and remediation of psycholinguistic disorders in chil-

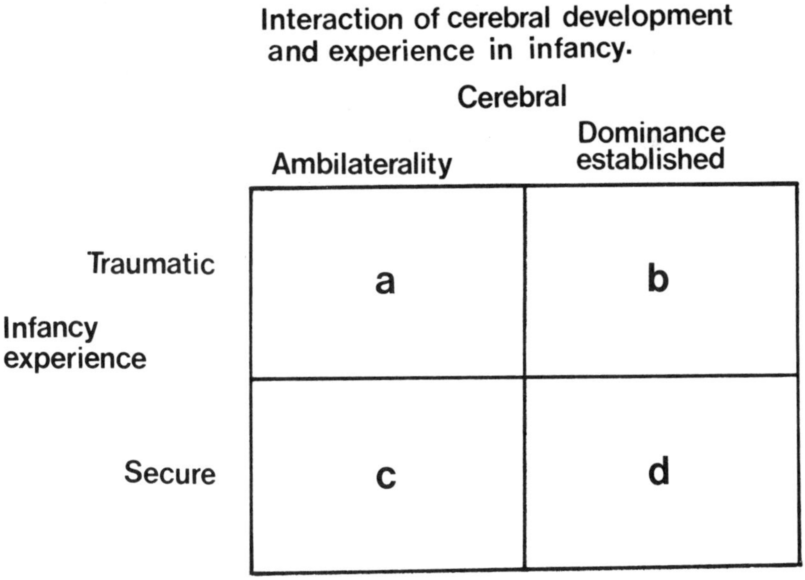

Interaction of cerebral development and experience in infancy.

	Cerebral Ambilaterality	Dominance established
Traumatic	**a**	**b**
Infancy experience		
Secure	**c**	**d**

Figure 11
Interaction of Cerebral Development and Experience in Infancy

dren" (Kirk and McLeod, 1966). The fact that a multiplicity of researchers have administered the test to unselected samples of children and have correlated psycholinguistic age with scores on reading or other tests either to investigate the concurrent overall relationship or to predict future performance across the educational board is their privilege, but of doubtful relevance to the clinically analytical purpose for which the test was designed. If correlations based on unselected populations are found are of "low practical significance," and criticized as such, it is rather like training an athlete for the 100 meter sprint and criticizing his performance when he fails in the 1500 meter race or, changing the metaphor, the authors have put up a straw man and proceeded to shoot him down.

But what constitutes a correlation coefficient that is of low practical significance? The authors arbitrarily set 0.35 as the cut-off for practical usefulness (without considering the effects of any attenuation). Figure 10 represents a "normal" sample of subjects for whom there is zero correlation between variables X and Y and a minority group who score low on both variables X and Y with a significant correlation (of 0.5) between X and Y. For a minority sample of 5 per cent of the population, the product-moment correlation for the total combined samples cannot rise to more than about 0.22.

The Validity of Head Counts

The authors have done a thorough job of searching the literature. However, although Gallup Polls provide generally valid evidence about the probable outcome of elections, they do not necessarily guarantee us adequate national leaders, nor do TV ratings guarantee us intelligent programming even though they do presumably reflect popular taste. In other words, the quality of a good deal of what passes for research (and I have had several years of experience as consulting editor to educational journals) does not inspire sufficient confidence to accept a simple head count as compellingly persuasive.

The Effect of Intelligence

On many occasions, the authors emphasize the virtue of "controlling for the effects of mental ability." Mercifully, they appear to be referring to the need to covary for IQ and not to match individuals for IQ (which thereby destroys the randomization theory basis on which most experimental designs are based). But why the insistence on this control? The only valid reason is that, if someone comes along with a new diagnostic device, it is reasonable to require that it does something over and above what we already have. Even this argument is debatable, if the new instrument does a comparable job of discrimination in terms that are clinically more intelligible than the existing instrument. But I suspect that the reason for the requirement that "intelligence must be controlled" is because, as Hunt (1961) has reminded us, we have been brainwashed into accepting the mystique and prepotency of whatever it is that intelligence tests measure. It is difficult to avoid reflecting that if a stranger from Mars—or even from the physical sciences—were to encounter an experimental situation where Test A (IQ) and Test B (ITPA) were being compared, and where the researcher evaluates Test B in terms of how well it discriminates between two groups of subjects after the effects of Test A had been eliminated, he might well ask "Why don't you evaluate the validity of Test A after you have allowed for the groups' differential performance on Test B?" What *is* the effectiveness of the WISC in discriminating young children with learning disabilities, after covarying for ITPA?

The Reported Study of Academic Correlates of Academic Achievement

The study is reported only sketchily and, while it was purportedly carefully designed so as to avoid some of the difficulties found in the reviewed research, it appears to have more than restored the balance by introducing several difficulties of its own. For instance, as the children came from Chester County, Pennsylvania, and their ages ranged from 105 to 118 months (average 112 months), they appear to be the same children as formed the basis of the study reported by Newcomer et al. (1974). If this is so, it is rather remarkable that there were thirty fewer children, despite the same chronological age characteristics, and that a short form of the ITPA was administered although the published article (Newcomer, 1974) states simply that "all children were administered the ITPA" (p. 509). Why were not the complete test data used in the presently reported study if they were available? We are told that the reliability and validity of the shortened version were acceptable, but the 1973 Newcomer reference is missing and there is no mention of reliability or validity of a shortened ITPA in the 1974 reference.

Moreover, although the unsupported assertion is made regarding the short form procedure "which ensured the applicability of the ITPA with children of this age" (p. 56), the short answer is that the procedure does not. As the sample contained children as old as nine years, ten months and the IQ range was 87 to 111, then inevitably many if not most of the children were in the upper reaches of the

ITPA norms, where discriminatory power falls off, and quite a few must have been at or beyond the ceiling of several subtests. It would have been more enlightening to have been furnished with the non-adjusted subtest means instead of, or in addition to, the adjusted means of table 9. From the information that is provided, however, we apparently have a group of average children at the upper age limit of the ITPA's range who are administered a shortened version of the ITPA, divided into three subgroups according to academic achievement, and academic achievement of the groups is correlated with performance on each modified ITPA subtest, after partialling out the effect of measured intelligence. One is compelled to agree with the authors that the three covariance analyses that achieved statistical significance were probably chance findings, for it would have been a miracle if anything significant had emerged. But the fault was hardly demonstrated to be in the ITPA.

Chapter 4 returns to a sound basic analysis of assumptions which underlie psycholinguistic remedial training programs. Research findings concerning the beneficial effects of psycholinguistic re-mediation have been less spectacular than had been optimistically hoped for in the 1960s. The authors appear to conclude on the basis of their assessment of ITPA test reliability and validity as adequate, that the underlying model, philosophy, and rationale must be at fault. The present reviewer would be more inclined not to reject alternative explanations, which the authors do review and recognize, namely that the methodology and adequacy of many of the reported training programs might be open to criticism and that some psycholinguistic skills—particularly at the automatic level—are particularly resistant to amelioration. With regard to this latter hypothesis, automatic level skills are those which are normally learned by the majority of children by repetitive experience, i.e., by the law of frequency rather than by the law of insight. Remediation of these skills is therefore particularly frustrating in that drill, in one form or another, is indicated, yet repetitive activity is inherently low in motivating power and learning disabled children, by their de-ficiencies in automatic level skills, have shown themselves to be less than susceptible to its effect.

If one elects to decide, contrary to the authors, that the ITPA subtests are *not* as valid or reliable as one would hope, and the pattern of performance on the subtests has formed the basis of remedial programming, then the authors' conclusion that the un-derlying model and rationale is invalid, is reversed—or at any rate not proven. In any event, the spontaneous and widespread welcome by clinicians—some of them hard-nosed clinicians—of the original experimental edition of the ITPA, helps to reinforce the contention that reaction to the published research on remediation (which does have some bright spots, as the chapter 4 review shows) should not be the summary rejection of model, test, and remedial programs but, as the authors state in their final paragraph, the cautious appraisal and monitoring of programs and, this reviewer would hope, a progressive sharpening of diagnostic instrumentation, the development of better field tested remedial strategies and methods, and, last but not least, an improvement in professional personnel development.

Dr. Hammill and his various associates have provided a useful service over the past few years in taking a good hard look at some of the currently fashionable cults that have been adopted too uncritically in remedial and special education. It would be unfortunate if their worthy endeavors were to degenerate—or to be perceived as degenerating—into mere iconoclasm and helping to demolish in the process a few icons that maybe needed some restoration, but whose destruction would not be in the best interests of the children whom we serve.

Reaction to Dr. McLeod's Viewpoint

We are delighted that Dr. McLeod's rebuttal provides us with the opportunity to isolate and discuss the principle objections which advocates of psycholinguistic approaches in education express when they are confronted with what must appear to be a vigorous challenge to many of their professional opinions on this subject. It is certainly true that most of us are resistant to new information which happens to fly in the face of our beliefs and that as a result we can generate readily a good deal of indignation toward those who insist upon reiterating those unwelcomed points. It is with full understanding of this fact that we can smile at Dr. McLeod's introductory comments referring to parts of our work as being superficial, simplistic, grandiose, and verbose, and respond to his more cogent and specific criticisms of our work.

In his discussion, Dr. McLeod seems to be saying that he too has misgivings about the statistical adequacy of the ITPA, especially the 1968 revision, but retains full confidence in the value of the Osgood-Kirk model (modified to include certain of Wepman's constructs), when it is used as a frame of reference for approaching the diagnosis of children with learning problems. His appreciation for this particular model is based primarily upon his own research (1965, 1968) and on that of Hart (1963) and has remained fully established with him throughout the years. Dr. McLeod's concern about the ITPA is apparent in his comments regarding the subtest reliabilities, which he suggests are too low to permit profile analysis, and in his concluding inference that the overall negative findings reported in chapters 3 and 4 might be caused by the fact that "the ITPA subtests are not as valid or reliable as one would hope." Although he has certain reservations about the ITPA, he cautions us not to throw out the baby (i.e., the Osgood-Kirk-Wepman model) with the bathwater (i.e., the ITPA).

Dr. McLeod knows full well that if the ITPA subtests can be taken as legitimate representations of the underlying model (which we suspect that for the most part they can) and if they are sufficiently reliable for use in research projects (which we assert that they are), then the results of the cumulative literature *may* indeed reflect upon the model itself.

To protect his Osgood-Kirk-Wepman rationale, Dr. McLeod maintains that the findings of most of the existent validity research, excepting his own of course (a forgivable bias to which most of us are guilty from time to time) should be either disregarded or at least viewed with suspicion. He bases this opinion regarding the inadequacies of the literature, especially that reviewed in chapter 3, on the suppositions that many of the investigators were incompetent in that:

1. They founded their efforts on "simplistic notions of diagnosis";
2. They were "graduate students in search of a thesis or researchers in search of a project" and that they might not have known how to administer or interpret the ITPA properly;
3. They used subjects who were too old;
4. They used the ITPA in a manner for which it was never intended, i.e., to predict academic achievement;
5. They employed inappropriate statistical procedures, e.g., correlation.

Since they are the basis of his rebuttal, we intend to respond to each of these points, then turn our attention to several of his less critical remarks which pertain to our own study and to various aspects of chapter 1, i.e., currently prevalent psycholinguistic theory, and chapter 2, i.e., questions of factoral research, test reliability, etc.

The research is based on simplistic notions of diagnosis. Relative to this point, we choose not to respond to the question of whether or not our notions concerning diagnosis, or those of some fifty other individuals, are in fact simplistic or complex according to Dr. McLeod's standards. Even if inclined to discuss such matters, we could not do so because we are not entirely sure what Dr. McLeod means when he refers to the "simplistic notions" of other professionals. In any event, philosophy of assessment is not the issue here. The issue is whether or not the findings of the correlational and diagnostic studies discussed in chapter 3 can be used to determine the value or lack of value of the ITPA when it is used for educational purposes.

The researchers might not have known how to administer the ITPA properly. We certainly question both Dr. McLeod's assumption that the ITPA was improperly administered in the vast majority of the studies which we have reviewed, and his conclusion that tester incompetence distorts the results of the accumulated research findings. In the first place, there is no reason to assume that the ITPA was administered inaccurately. Just to infer that it *might have been* poorly administered is not the same as showing that it *was*. As a matter of fact, there is some indirect evidence which would indicate that the ITPA was indeed administered properly in the studies which we reviewed. Let us assume, for the moment, that some of the investigators were more likely than others to have given the ITPA correctly, e.g., those trained or supervised by professionals who are closely associated with the ITPA or psycholinguistic approaches to education. By comparing the results of their studies to those reported by the other researchers, we might determine if any appreciable differences exist between them.

Investigators who studied the ITPA's diagnostic validity (see table 6) who we would expect to have been trained to administer the test properly were Elkins (1972), a student of Dr. McLeod's, and Kass (1966), a student of Dr. Samuel Kirk's. Investigators who studied the effects of psycholinguistic training (see table 12) who seem likely to know how to administer the ITPA were Karnes (1970), Painter (1966), and Wiseman (1965), all students of Kirk's; and Minskoff (1965), now a coauthor of the MWM psycholinguistic training program and at one time a master's degree student of Kirk's.

Inspection of the results of these studies, as presented in the respective tables, is sufficient to indicate that their findings are essentially the same as those reported in the rest of the research literature. Therefore, there is no tangible evidence upon which to base the assertion that the cumulative findings of the research reported in chapters 3 and 4 should be discredited in any way because the researchers involved did not know how to administer the test properly.

The subjects used were too old.   Another "shortcoming" which Dr. McLeod points out is that the investigators used subjects who were too old and as a result might have scored above the upper threshold of the ITPA subtests, thereby producing ceiling effects in their data. In such cases, the resultant coefficients between the ITPA subtests and the various measures of academic skills would appear to be much lower than would be the case if the range of ITPA scores extended to the upper limits of the child's psycholinguistic competence. In other words, the upper limits of the test would simply cut off their scores and make them appear to resemble children with less psycholinguistic ability. If this were the case, the uncritical acceptance of such a statistic would indeed be unfortunate, for the coefficient might or might not reflect the true state of the relationship. Yet, we seriously doubt if ceiling effects had any appreciable influence on the results of the correlational studies which we reviewed because in twenty of twenty-nine investigations, the age of the subjects ranged from five through eight. There can be no real question of ceiling effects within this age interval, since the original ITPA was standardized for use with children as old as 9–3, and the revised test extended the age ceiling to 10–3. In an additional three of these studies, the subjects were intellectually retarded and doubtlessly had mental ages well below nine on the average.

Dr. McLeod's concern regarding the possible ceiling effects in the study which we undertook and reported in chapter 3 is without any foundation, for the *oldest* subjects in the sample were only 9 years, 10 months, of age, five months below the upper age level for using the test. Just to be sure that ceiling effects were not present in the data, we inspected the raw scores and found that they were more or less normally distributed with no more than the expected number of children reaching the test's ceiling. For example, on Auditory Sequential Memory, only two of the 138 subjects scored in the 50s; the ceiling for this subtest is 56.

In addition we were able to acquire the raw data used by Larsen, Sowell, and Rogers, who also employed nine-year-old children as subjects and found that ceiling effects were not present in their study either. Therefore, in at least twenty-five of the twenty-nine studies, there is no reason for believing that ceiling effects caused the generally unsupportive conclusions concerning the ITPA. Suppositions to the contrary simply cannot be taken seriously.

The ITPA was never intended to predict academic achievement. Dr. McLeod's fourth major criticism is that the researchers in studying the relationship between the ITPA and various academic variables have in some way missed the whole point of the test and consequently have asked the wrong questions. He asserts that "the ITPA was developed as a practical clinical procedure for the diagnosis and remediation of *psycholinguistic disorders* (our italics) in children" and as a result the accumulated correlational research which studied the relationship to *academic performance* is of little relevance.

Whether the ITPA was intended to be used as an adjunct for academic instruction or as only a test of psycholinguistic abilities is quite immaterial, for both we and Dr. McLeod know that in practice the ITPA is used with underachieving school-aged children for the following reasons: to acquire information which can be used to explain the cause of their academic problems, to identify the pupil's "preferred learning style," and/or to plan "appropriate" instructional programs which will have a pay-off in increased achievement in reading, spelling, arithmetic, etc.

Educators have good reason for using the ITPA in this manner because they are encouraged to do so by Kirk and Kirk (1971), Minskoff, Wiseman, and Minskoff (1972), Bush and Giles (1969), and by almost all other advocates of psycholinguistic approaches in education. The sheer weight of the research which deals with the relationship of the test to academic subject matter testifies in part to the way in which the test is actually used in the schools. As this is the real situation in the schools, it seems inappropriate to criticize as "inappropriate" the efforts of individuals to determine the precise correlation between the ITPA and measures of academic abilities. Certainly such research attempts should not be arbitrarily dismissed as mere "straw-man" efforts.

Correlation is an inappropriate statistic. Dr. McLeod's last major point is that there are inherent problems in using correlation to study the relationship between the ITPA and academic performance. He points out that for any group of children the correlation coefficient depicting the relationship between two variables might be $r = 0$, while for a subgroup within the group the relationship between the variables might be $r = .5$ (see figure 10). In other words, the correlation literature should be disregarded or at the very least minimized because it has not been conducted with appropriate samples of children; presumably there is a segment of children whose school failure is caused by or associated with psycholinguistic deficits but the relationship is obscured by the fact that they constitute a small portion within a larger sample.

This is an argument which is frequently used against correlational statistical procedures, but it is easier to hypothesize that this *may be* the case than it is to demonstrate that it *is* the case. Perhaps the advocates of psycholinguistic approaches in education should define the characteristics of this presumed subgroup, find an appropriate sample of children, and implement a correctional study to test their theory. Such evidence would certainly add credence to their argument. Until this is done, however, we see no reason to arbitrarily disregard the results of the cumulated correlational research.

Dr. McLeod also challenges the importance we gave to controlling for the effects of mental ability in the correlational research. Our particular concern with this dimension is not due to his "only valid reason," i.e., that the ITPA must do something over and above what an intelligence test does. We simply wanted to know if it is doing something *different* than an intelligence test does—something which is unique to psycholinguistics. For example, if the research appears to demonstrate a relatively high correlative relationship between a particular subtest, e.g., Grammatic Closure, and tests of academic achievement, important information is gained when the potency of this relationship is evaluated by controlling for the variable of mental ability. To those individuals who would refute this technique as unnatural because mental ability is an integral component of all human behavior, we can only suggest that they are free to consider the accumulated research which did *not* control the intelligence factor (see tables 7 and 8). As one can tell from a quick perusal of those tables, the results are not particularly significant whether or not IQ is controlled for.

It was to some extent in anticipation that these arguments might be directed against the use of correlation that prompted us to analyze the twenty-four diagnostic studies. The rationale for these investigations is quite different from those which used correlation, though the studies provide answers to the same question, i.e., what is the educational significance of the ITPA? In these investigations the ITPA performance of a group of children which is experiencing some type of learning problem such as reading failure is compared with the ITPA performance of a group which is progressing well in reading. If there really is a subgroup of children in school whose academic problems are caused by or associated with psycholinguistic deficits and whose presence is obscured in the correlational research, they should certainly be discovered in these studies.

The results of these investigations are summarized in table 7 and certainly provide the ITPA advocates with little encouragement. Few of the subtests consistently discriminate between groups. Such research is particularly credible for none of the arguments directed against the correlational research is appropriately applied here. In fact, the conclusions relating to our review of the diagnostic literature, which incidently was largely ignored by Dr. McLeod, leads one to wonder what evidence the sophisticated clinician requires before he begins to question his notions. Where are these elusive children whose learning problems are related to the ITPA-defined deficits? If the subtests do not correlate at significant levels with reading, spelling, arithmetic, etc., and if they do not discriminate between children who are good or poor in those abilities, what are they good for in education?

In addition to discussing the shortcomings in the literature in general, Dr. McLeod directs several criticisms specifically to the study which we reported in chapter 3. We intend to respond to these at this time. First, he asks why 167 subjects were used in the construct validity study (Newcomer et al., 1974) and only *138* were used in the correlation-diagnostic validity study, if these two studies used the sample of children. The discrepancy is easily explained by the fact that only 138 subjects attended schools which routinely administered the California Achievement Tests, the criterion variable in the latter study. The twenty-nine "missing" subjects were not dropped from the sample after the fact; they were simply not included at all in the second study.

Second, he takes us to task for not correcting the coefficients reported in table 8 for attenuation, a criticism which has some validity. This statistical procedure results in an adjustment in the size of the coefficients to account for the reliability in the predictor variable, the criterion variable, or both. In response to Dr. McLeod's comments, we applied the correction to the coefficients reported in table 8. Since we were concerned only with the practical validity of the ITPA subtests as predictors of academic subjects, the formula recommended for this purpose by Guilford (1959, p. 477) was used, a procedure which corrects for attenuation in the criterion variable only.

The technique made no appreciable difference when applied to the coefficients from which the influence of IQ had been partialled. Regarding the coefficients which had not been corrected for IQ effects, however, three coefficients were raised to .35, the minimum level of practical usefulness (two related to AR and 1 to VC). Therefore, even when the procedures used maximized the size of the coefficients, i.e., when the IQ is *not* partialled and when the correction for attenuation *is made*, the coefficients depicting the relationship between the ITPA subtests and measures of reading, spelling, and arithmetic fail to reach the .35 level for eight of the twelve subtests (VE, ME, ASM, VSM, VA, VR, AC, and SB).

Third, the comments made by Dr. McLeod regarding our use of a shortened version of the ITPA in this study require some explanation to set the record straight. In the Hare et al. (1973) and the Newcomer et al. (1974) factor analytic-construct validity studies, three subtests were administered in their entirety (ASM, VSM, VR). The remaining subtests were split into two forms. The first kept the regular ITPA format; the other presented the items using a different modality of input or output. For example, half of the items on Auditory Reception were administered in the standard fashion and half were read by the child who circled "yes" or "no" on an answer sheet. This procedure made it possible to develop true criterion tasks which shared the same content and varied only on the dimension of channel. These were originally used in the construct validity articles; the same data were used later in the educational usefulness study which was discussed in chapter 3 and explains why the shortened version of the ITPA was used. The reliabilities for these altered tests should have been included in the text of this book or at least a proper reference to them (Newcomer, 1973) should have been provided. Our apologies to Dr. McLeod. Incidently, the reliabilities for those *shortened* tests are approximately equal to or greater than those reported in the test manual with the exception of that for Visual Association which is somewhat lower.

Having dealt with the most essential part of Dr. McLeod's rebuttal, we can discuss several of his other remarks. Regarding chapter 1, "Application of Psycholinguistics to Education," he recommends including a discussion of Chomsky's later works. From our point of view, further elaboration of Chomsky's evolving position was neither necessary nor helpful since the point was to introduce the most dominant alternative to Osgood's frame of reference, not to engage in a discussion of the state-of-the-art in psycholinguistics. It was also outside our stated purpose to discuss the ongoing research in psycholinguistics. We do insist, however, that insofar as modern psycholinguistic theory is concerned, those particular contributions of Osgood which underlie the development of the ITPA are no longer considered important (McNeill, 1970), and that was our main point.

Regarding chapter 2, "The Illinois Test of Psycholinguistic Abilities," Dr. McLeod raises questions relating to three issues: (1) our familiarity with the ITPA, (2) our failure to include a review of the factor analytic research, and (3) our willingness to accept the ITPA subtests as reliable measures. In his first point, Dr. McLeod suggests that "the authors are less intimately acquainted with the test than might be expected from someone engaged in a critical analysis." He bases this remark on the fact that several of the examples which we gave to illustrate the content of the ITPA subtests were not actually items which appear in the subtests. While it is true that we simply invented several typical ITPA-type items as examples, it is not true that we were unaware that they were not actual test items. We really did administer the test in the studies which we reported, and we are quite familiar with its contents.

Regarding his second point, we can understand Dr. McLeod's surprise over our failure to include an extensive review of the ITPA factor analytic research in our book. As we were interested in the ITPA's construct validity, we initially considered including this information. After reviewing the literature, however, we noted that few of the available studies utilized alternate reference tests specifically designed to measure the same constructs which are supposedly tapped by the ITPA. At this point we accepted the position of Proger, Cross, and Burger (1973, p. 182) that such analyses (*sans* appropriate reference tests) would likely lead to erroneous conclusions regarding the ITPA's construct validity. Therefore, we regarded the prevalent conclusions emerging from this literature, i.e., that the ITPA lacks construct validity, as being inconclusive and possibly misleading, and decided not to discuss the topic at great length.

Since Dr. McLeod has raised the point and referred to the review of factor analytic research reported by Sedlack and Weener (1973) in Mann and Sabatino's *First Review of Special Education*, we feel justified in noting their conclusion. They state that "the tentative factors that have been identified in factor analytic studies offer scant support for the channel-level-process modes on which the ITPA is based" (p. 124).

Dr. McLeod and others might well reflect on the meaning of this last statement regarding the validity of the test and/or the model. The Sedlack and Weener conclusions might be interpreted several ways:

1. Since the channel-level-process dimensions on the ITPA were not substantiated in the factor analytic research, it is obvious that the test bears little similarity to the model upon which it was supposedly based; therefore the results of studies which used the test do not reflect on the model, or

2. Since the ITPA was built in fact using the model as a guide, the lack of support for the channel-level-process dimensions does reflect on the validity of the model to some extent.

The truth may be that the model is valid theoretically but represents dimensions which are too complex and intertwined to be operationalized either in a test or in a teacher's clinical judgment.

In his third point relating to material in chapter 2, Dr. McLeod expresses surprise that we appear "to be more sanguine than Kirk and Paraskevopoulos about the test's reliability." All we can do here is to reiterate our earlier comments concerning reliability, i.e., that the internal consistency reliabilities of the subtests seem to be adequate (greater than .80) and that test-retest reliability has not been sufficiently explored to permit the formulation of definitive statements. On the question of reliability, Dr. McLeod goes well beyond us and asserts, perhaps correctly, that because of the way in which the test is used, i.e., the results of the subtests are used to profile a child's ability across various psycholinguistic constructs, the ITPA reliabilities should be even higher than those associated with the subtests of the Wechsler Intelligence Scale for Children; but, of course, he points out that they are not higher than those of the WISC. We can also appreciate that Dr. McLeod would be very concerned about the absence of convincing ITPA test-retest reliability data, for this kind of reliability is of utmost importance for clinicians and teachers.

While tentatively agreeing with Dr. McLeod that the reliabilities of the ITPA subtests might be too low for profiling an individual's psycholinguistic deficits and strengths, we do assert strongly that the internal consistency reliabilities are quite adequate for use in the research projects which we reviewed, for they are concerned with group, rather than individual, performance. As internal consistency coefficients greater than .80 are without doubt sufficient for most research purposes, the rather discouraging findings reported in chapters 3 and 4 cannot be dismissed on the argument that the ITPA subtests lack sufficient reliability.

To conclude, we applaud Dr. McLeod's statement that a child's ITPA test performance can lead to inappropriate instructional prescriptions. We disagree, however, that this necessarily occurs because of inadequate teacher preparation. No matter how sophisticated or creative a teacher might be in her diagnostic teaching efforts, her effectiveness will be reduced if she bases any part of her programs on invalid information, i.e., the ITPA subtest results which as yet have no proven relationship to school achievement. This point is in fact what chapter 3 says and what many psycholinguistic, ITPA–oriented clinicians continue to deny. Simply stated, the subtests do not appear to be related significantly to academic achievement; they do not even consistently discriminate between good and poor achievers. Until it can be demonstrated with empirical consistency that the ITPA is a viable, predictive, and diagnostically useful instrument, and the advocates of psycholinguistic approaches *cannot* do so at this point in time, we have no recourse other than to accept the existent research and to recommend a moratorium on the use of this test to obtain educationally useful information.

What does all of this have to do with determining the validity of the Osgood-Kirk-Wepman model? The answer to that question will depend upon the reader's evaluation of the material presented in chapter 3, Dr. McLeod's rebuttal, and our response. For example:

1. If the reader accepts the ITPA as a reliable and valid representation of the model and rejects the research literature as inappropriate and full of errors, he will conclude that the educational usefulness of neither the test nor the model have been fairly evaluated. In other words, neither are validated.

2. If the reader agrees with Dr. McLeod, that the ITPA may be insufficient to test the educational importance of the model, he will interpret the cumulated research as having relevance only for the test and conclude that the ITPA is not useful for educational practice. He would draw no adverse conclusions regarding the model upon which the test is based. This position would mean, of course, that the clinical application of this widely employed diagnostic model is actually nonvalidated at the present time.

3. If the reader accepts the ITPA as a reliable and valid representation of the model and accepts the cumulative findings of the research, he will conclude that both the ITPA and its model have little relevance for academic performance.

In a sense, whether one agrees with Dr. McLeod or with us is actually immaterial as far as the ITPA's educational value is concerned. Our differences center on the value of the model for instructional purposes, not on the value of the test. Dr. McLeod accepts the model, questions the ITPA, and dismisses the cumulative research. We, on the other hand, question the model, dismiss the ITPA, and yield to the cumulative research findings, at least regarding educational matters. As Dr. McLeod apparently agrees with us that the ITPA itself has little relevance for instruction of school subjects, we presume that his interest in pointing out these supposed shortcomings in the validity of ITPA research methodology is intended for the reader's edification, rather than as a serious challenge to our basic conclusion concerning the ITPA's educational usefulness.

Permit us one final comment. As to Dr. McLeod's concern over throwing the baby out with the bathwater, we can say only that we too are opposed to child abuse and resist any hasty, unwarranted acts which might have adverse effects upon any kind of infant. On the other hand, isn't it incumbent upon the advocates of psycholinguistic based training to demonstrate through carefully designed and replicated research that there are in fact babies in the bathwater?

6

Summary and Concluding Remarks

Thus far in this book we have (1) provided the reader with a brief introduction to the field of psycholinguistics, (2) discussed in more detail a particular psycholinguistic theory which has been applied widely in education, i.e., the Kirk adaptation of the Osgood Model, (3) assembled and interpreted the presently available empirical evidence regarding the effectiveness of those tests and training programs which are based on that model, (4) provided a forum for the advocates of this approach to rebut our conclusions or state their own positions, and (5) responded to their statements.

Up to this point, we have endeavored to limit our comments to interpretations of the research studies which we have reviewed. Although our study of the data has caused us to assume what is essentially a nonadvocacy stance regarding most aspects of psycholinguistics as applied in education today, we have attempted to avoid excessive comment regarding the theoretical and philosophical issues which underlie these psycholinguistic activities. We would now like to depart momentarily from this, probably wise prohibition, and discuss several of our concerns which are of a philosophical nature.

We must admit that as we have read and reviewed the books and materials authored by those who advocate the use of ITPA-like psycholinguistic models, we have been struck by the lack of clarity and the disagreement among their positions regarding several important philosophical issues which, in our opinion, are basic to their work. We refer primarily to their conceptualizations regarding the processes which they maintain are responsible for psycholinguistic learning. Specifically, we are confused as to what the proponents of the Kirk-Osgood model mean when they refer to "auditory reception," "visual memory," "verbal expression," "representational level," etc. Seemingly they differ markedly among themselves in the manner in which they interpret these terms.

On the one hand, certain of their number appear to accept Osgood's and Kirk's theoretical postulations quite literally. Osgood, of course, clearly delineates his constructs as designators of *actual mental functions* within the brain. As a behavioral psychologist applying a stimulus-response paradigm to explain learning, he hypothesizes the existence of fractional mediating responses within the central nervous system which permits the human organism to process and store language information, i.e., to acquire language. Viewed in this light, "auditory reception," for example, refers to the functioning of those particular neutral processes which are responsible for a person's ability to take in and to understand all types of verbal information, both meaningful and nonmeaningful.

Kirk, McCarthy, and Kirk seemingly adopt Osgood's philosophical position as well as his rationale for their test. They state quite clearly that the ITPA is designed for use with children who have specific learning disabilities, i.e., those who exhibit a disorder in one or more of the basic psychological processes involved in understanding or using spoken or written language, including conditions previously referred to as perceptual handicaps, brain injury, minimal brain dysfunction, dyslexia, developmental aphasia, and so forth. In other words, the ITPA is designed to measure the disordered processes which cause these conditions. To Kirk and his colleagues the terms "auditory reception," "verbal expression," "visual sequential memory," etc., very definitely refer to inferred psychoneurological processes which operate within the brain. Although Kirk is perhaps more psychological and less neurological in his focus and choice of terminology than is Osgood, he essentially seems convinced that Osgood's conceptualizations represent actual mental operations or functions.

An alternate position regarding the nature of these psycholinguistic processes is that they simply represent hypothesized constructs, rather than actual neural functions; and, as such, they may be conveniently employed to label and group various behaviors. The individuals adhering to this position, including to varying degrees Drs. Minskoff, Bush, and McLeod, regard the model as being most valuable when it is used as a "frame of reference" or as a "linguistic convenience" to facilitate communication among professionals. From this point of view, terms such as "auditory reception" are generic labels representing superordinate categories under which countless subordinate behaviors can be assembled. These subordinate behaviors may be grouped together because they all satisfy a common definition, rather than because they have a similar neurological foundation. For example, such apparently different tasks as discrimination among pure tone sounds, comprehending a conversation, and recognizing verbally presented absurdities are readily identified as belonging to the "auditory reception" category because they all involve, in some manner, the ability to understand what is heard. Those who regard the model as a "frame of reference" apparently chose to ignore the theoretical implications expressed in the work of Osgood or Kirk, and make few statements about training underlying psychoneurological processes.

In practice, however, whether one believes that the constructs of the model actually represent specific mental functions or that they are simply labels for related behaviors seems to make little difference. Advocates of both positions accept the assumption that the Osgood-Kirk premises have unprecedented usefulness in education. They generally adhere to the format and terminology of the model when diagnosing and describing children's learning problems. Second, they accept the concept that the underlying psycholinguistic abilities may be trained; and, third, they share the belief that such training will increase a child's capacity to learn academic content.

The relatively unmitigated application of the model in diagnosis by adherents of both orientations, generally results in the formulation of global generalizations regarding children's learning deficits. For example, they use a child's performance on the ITPA, various psycholinguistic checklists, etc., as a basis for diagnosing a general deficit in "auditory reception" or in any of the other eleven psycholinguistic abilities which are part of the ITPA model. In doing so, they imply that the few specific tasks which they used to make the general diagnosis, i.e., "auditory reception" deficit, are representative of the other tasks which are included in that particular category. Therefore, they would attribute commonality to tasks such as speech sound discrimination, memory for digits orally presented, and listening with comprehension because they all are considered "auditory reception" behaviors. A further example of the diagnostic application of the psychoneurological terminology associated with the dimensions of the model is seen in a description of a poor reader as having an auditory-visual integration problem at both the Representational and the Integrational levels which is associated with difficulties in auditory and visual sequential memory. The generalized use of these constructs as descriptors makes the advocates' convictions regarding their actual meaning irrelevant.

The second assumption, which by its acceptance appears to unite all who utilize the ITPA model format, relates to their basic approach to training. Their procedures in the assessment and identification of children's learning problems, as well as their attitudes toward program-planning and materials selection, suggest that they are governed by the idea that general, psychological abilities which underly all learning will be improved through instruction. In other words, if one assumes that "memory" is necessary for learning, then training "memory" will enhance all learning. Their approach, therefore, can be described as one in which general ability training, rather than specific task teaching, is emphasized.

This brings us to the last and a most important assumption which is shared by almost all of those who advocate the application of psycholinguistic models, i.e., their belief that training a child in the tasks related to the ITPA constructs or functions will not only improve his specific psycholinguistic deficits, but will in some way increase his ability to learn academic content as well. In other words, if a child's training in "auditory reception" is successful, he will not only experience improvement in that ability but he also will progress more satisfactorily in his attempts to learn to read, spell, do arithmetic, etc.

For the reasons just stated, it seems to us that whether an individual believes that the dimensions of the model represent frames of reference for behaviors or actual neural events is immaterial from a practical point of view, for his adherence to either position does not seem to affect the manner in which he applies the model to the diagnosis and remediation of children's learning problems. Yet the issue is one which warrants clarification since it influences the manner in which children's learning failures are conceptualized, not only by a particular diagnostician but also by other educators, parents, and, possibly, the children themselves.

Consider the case of a youngster who does poorly on the ITPA Auditory Reception subtest and who also is inept in comprehending orally presented stories, etc. Does the child's failure signify: (1) the presence of a deficit in the neural operations which underlie the function "auditory reception"; (2) the existence of an unusual number of problems within a construct or family of behaviors the parameters of which are set on the basis of an arbitrary definition and face validity; or (3) nothing more than the fact that the child is having difficulty in mastering two or three discrete behaviors which for descriptive purposes can be called "auditory reception" tasks? The answer given by any one diagnostician may depend in part upon how he has resolved the basic question: What do the components of the theoretical models mean to me?

The issue becomes even more perplexing in cases where remediation has been implemented "successfully." For example, assume that the child described in the previous paragraph was provided with training in "auditory reception" after which he passed the Auditory Reception subtest, responded appropriately to stories, etc. Would the teacher-clinician conclude: (1) that the neural processes or functions incorporated in "auditory reception" had been strengthened to the point where the child could now perform better those tasks which were dependent on these mental operations; (2) that by successfully teaching several "auditory reception" tasks, the child now had the "idea" and, therefore, would do well on other tasks encompassed within the definition of the construct; or (3) that the particular "auditory reception" tasks which improved were those which were systematically taught and no further inferences are made or considered proper? Once again, the answer would depend upon one's theoretical position on the basic issue concerning the nature of the model's dimensions.

We should reiterate at this point that although adequate explanations regarding the meaning of the constructs might influence attitudes toward particular children, we believe that all interpretations are subject to the same basic criticisms. It is our acceptance of the validity of these criticisms in conjunction with the cumulative results of the pertinent research presented previously which has led us to question the accuracy of the rationale offered by most advocates of psycholinguistic approaches in education.

First, the Osgood model, which is based on an appreciable amount of experimental psychology research, is simply a series of inferences regarding the mental processes which control learning. Theories of this sort are helpful in shedding light on the complexities of human information processing, and we certainly support the efforts of those who study them in order to increase their knowledge about learning. We must point out, however, that experimental psychologists and neurologists who specialize in investigating this area are currently unable to do much more than to formulate relatively primitive theories regarding brain functions. A major cause for this situation is that neural operations are so complex, closely interwoven, and interdependent that it is next to impossible to investigate them discretely. Highly sophisticated mathematical calculations can be used to identify seemingly discrete abilities, but this is done usually for the purposes of research or for theory building. Few researchers would assert that such statistically defined constructs would serve as the basis for diagnosing and treating the educational problems of individual children.

Second, we recognize that teaching a child a particular skill, such as the ability to solve verbal absurdities, might improve his competence at that task, but we suspect that it is considerably less likely that the specific mastery of this task will improve a general mental process within the brain, in this case "auditory reception." It is equally unlikely that the improvement will generalize to the performance of other tasks which are included under the heading of "auditory reception." To us, the ultimate in remote possibilities, however, is that the improvement in a specific "auditory reception" task, especially one like recognizing verbal absurdities, will somehow increase the child's capacity to perform academic tasks such as reading, spelling, or arithmetic.

A third and related point is that regardless of the extent to which psycholinguistic advocates attempt to connect the tasks, which they view as representing various psychological processes, to academic learning (i.e., to make them more educationally relevant), it seems to us that their efforts are likely to fail since they are based on unsubstantiated and possibly faulty assumptions. Not only is it unproven that the tasks which are part of each process area relate to each other in a manner which makes it legitimate to group them into the ITPA superordinate categories, but their relationship to academics is also doubtful. Consequently, training tasks which supposedly underlie academic learning will likely succeed only in wasting instructional effort. Simply stated, remedial teaching designed to improve academic achievement should relate to academics, e.g., reading skill might grow with tutoring in phonics, phoneme-grapheme correspondence, work attack skills, regardless of the psycholinguistic functions involved. However, instruction in skills which are not related to reading, but which are designed to strengthen "auditory reception" in the hope that increased "auditory reception" will contribute or generalize to achievement in reading, constitutes an "off-task" approach which educators can ill afford, if their goal is to teach reading. If on the other hand, their goal is simply to improve psycholinguistic competencies, with or without generalizations pertaining to the overall growth and development of psychological processes, they must demonstrate the value of remediating these particular specific skills. They must show how these activities make the child a more effective person since evidence accrued thus far would not support their position or is not available.

In the final analysis, the resolution of the philosophical questions pertaining to these psycholinguistic approaches may not matter one iota. The validity of the rationale behind the measurement and training of psycholinguistic abilities is a moot issue unless the advocates can demonstrate the educational usefulness of the original Osgood postulations, the Kirk adaptation of Osgood's model, the ITPA and/or the related training programs by showing that such approaches will indeed contribute to improving children's academic, linguistic, or social performance. A reading of the existent research raises serious questions in our minds concerning almost all aspects of current psycholinguistic practice; and we are unconvinced by the counterinterpretations of the research or the arguments made by Bush, Minskoff, or McLeod and others in defense of present day practices. The reader will simply have to make up his own mind.

We cannot conclude this chapter without referring the reader to Lester Mann's (1971) treatise, "Psychometric Phrenology and the New Faculty Psychology: The Case against Ability Assessment and Training," which deals with the philosophic and empiric shortcomings of ability training in general and of the ITPA-related approaches in particular. In this article, he points out that these approaches bear more than a little similarity to the long discredited "faculty psychology" ideas so prevalent during the 1800s and suggests that as applied in schools and clinics the approach may increase the danger in fractionalizing both the child and the way in which his problem is conceptualized. His assertions, however, are strongly challenged in rebuttals by Raymond Barsch, Jack Bardon, Archie Silver, Rosa Hagen, Edward Scagliotta, David Sabatino, and Morton Bortner who formulated cogent and occasionally powerful apologies for current attempts to train basic abilities. Mann's article and the responses directed to it appear in the winter-spring 1971 issue of the *Journal of Special Education*. This is a prime reference for readers who have an interest in the topic and should not be overlooked.

Probably our conclusions and opinions will have little influence on most teacher-clinicians who use these psycholinguistic approaches. Many, possibly most, of these professionals will simply dismiss our observations as the impractical ramblings of "ivory tower research-types." For the most part, they will continue to diagnose children using primarily the ITPA, match the resultant profiles with "appropriate" materials or activities, and train children utilizing this particular psycholinguistic model. If pressed for evidence to support their activities, many of them will undoubtedly do as they have done so often in the past, i.e., seek out those few studies which support their positions, disregard any methodological weaknesses in them, and quote the results to a public which lacks either the interest or the information to raise serious questions or objections.

We recognize that the results of future research, hopefully utilizing improved designs, may eventually validate the assumptions which are fundamental to psycholinguistic assessment and remediation. Conceivably, old programs and tests along with newly developed ones might be demonstrated, by research not yet completed or undertaken, to be instructionally useful. Should this prove to be the case, none will be more delighted than we. If such a happy event should occur, we would like to believe that our efforts, as exemplified by this book, had in some way served as a catalyst or stimulant to the initiation of the subsequent investigations. Awaiting the accumulation of future findings, however, we . . .

References

Anders, S. From a presentation in Hereford, Texas, October 1974.

Bannatyne, A., & Wichiarajote, P. Relationship between written spelling, motor functioning and sequencing skills. *Journal of Learning Disabilities*, 1969, **2**, 4–16.

Barritt, L. S., Semmel, M. I., & Weener, P. D. A comparison of the psycholinguistic functioning of educationally-deprived and educationally-advantaged children. Paper presented at the American Educational Research Association Meeting, Chicago, February 1966.

Bartin, N. The intellectual and psycholinguistic characteristics of three groups of differentiated third grade readers. Unpublished doctoral dissertation, State University of New York, Buffalo, 1971.

Bateman, B. *The Illinois Test of Psycholinguistic Abilities in current research*. Urbana, Ill.: Institute for Research on Children, University of Illinois Press, 1964.

_____. *The Illinois Test of Psycholinguistic Abilities in current research: Summaries of studies*. Urbana, Ill.: University of Illinois Press, 1965.

_____. Reading and psycholinguistic processes of partially seeing children. *CEC Research Monographs*, Series A, No. 5, 1963.

Bateman, B., & Wetherell, J. Psycholinguistic aspects of mental retardation. *Mental Retardation*, 1965, **3**, 8–13.

163

Bender, L. Communication in children with developmental alexia. In P. H. Hock, & J. Zubin (Eds.), *Psychopathology of communication*. New York: Grune & Stratton, 1958.

Berko, J. The child's learning of English morphology. *Word*, 1958, **14**, 150–77.

Bilovsky, D., & Share, J. ITPA and Down's syndrome: An exploratory study. *American Journal of Mental Deficiency*, 1965, **70**, 78–82.

Blessing, K. R. An investigation of a psycholinguistic deficit in educable mentally retarded children: Detection, remediation, and related variables. Unpublished doctoral dissertation, University of Wisconsin, Madison. *International Dissertation Abstracts*, 1964, **25**, 2327.

Blue, C. The effectiveness of a group language program with trainable mentally retarded children. *Education and Training for the Mentally Retarded*, 1970, **5**, 109–112.

Boden, E. Developmental dyslexia: A diagnostic approach based on three atypical reading-spelling patterns. *Developmental Medical Child Neurology*, 1973, **15**, 663–87.

Bowlby, J., Ainsworth, M., Boston, M., & Rosenbluth, D. The effects of mother-child separation: A follow-up study. *British Journal of Medical Psychology*, 1956, **29**, 211–47.

Bradley, B. H., Maurer, R., & Hundzial, M. A study of the effectiveness of milieu therapy and language training for the mentally retarded. *Exceptional Children*, 1966, **33**, 143–49.

Brown, L. F., & Rice, J. A. Psycholinguistic differentiation of low IQ children. *Mental Retardation*, 1967, **5**, 16–20.

Bruininks, R. H. Auditory and visual perceptual skills related to the reading performance of disadvantaged boys. *Perceptual and Motor Skills*, 1969, **29**, 177–86.

Bruininks, R. H., Lucker, W. G., & Gropper, R. Psycholinguistic abilities of good and poor reading disadvantaged first-graders. *Elementary School Journal*, 1970, **70**, 378–86.

Bruner, J. S., Oliver, R. R., Greenfield, P. M., et al. *Studies into cognitive growth*. New York: Wiley, 1966.

Burns, G. W. Factor analysis of the revised ITPA with underachieving children. *Journal of Learning Disabilities*, 1973, **6**, 371–76.

Bush, W. J., & Giles, M. T. *Aids to psycholinguistic teaching*. Columbus, Ohio: Charles E. Merrill, 1969.

Bush, W. J., & Gregg, D. K. Some interactions between individual differences and modes of instruction. Fairborn, Ohio: Aerospace Medical Research Laboratories, Aerospace Medical Division, Air Force Systems Command, Wright Patterson Air Force Base, 1965.

Butts, T. M. A study of race and social class variables and psycholinguistic, cognitive, and perceptual measures of selected first grade children. Unpublished doctoral dissertation, University of Alabama, Tuscaloosa. Ann Arbor, Mich.: University Microfilms, 1970, No. 71–9063.

Caccamo, J. M., & Yater, A. C. The ITPA and Negro children with Down's syndrome. *Exceptional Children*, 1972, **38**, 642–43.

Caldwell, B. M. A decade of early intervention programs: What we have learned. *American Journal of Orthopsychiatry*, 1974, **44**, 491–96.

Carrow, M. A. The development of auditory comprehension of language structure in children. *Journal of Speech and Hearing Disorders*, 1968, **33**, 99–111.

Carter, J. L. The effect of a group language stimulation program upon Negro culturally disadvantaged first grade children. Unpublished doctoral dissertation, University of Texas, Austin, 1966. *See also*: The effect of a language stimulation program upon first grade educationally disadvantaged children. *Education and Training for the Mentally Retarded*, 1966, **1**, 169–74.

Cartwright, G. P., & Cartwright, C. A. Gilding the lily: Comments on the training based model. *Exceptional Children*, 1972, **39**, 231–34.

Chomsky, C. *The acquisition of syntax in children from five to ten*. Cambridge, Mass.: MIT Press, 1969.

Chomsky, N. *Syntactic structures*. The Hague: Mouton, 1957.

_____. *Aspects of the theory of syntax*. The Hague: Mouton, 1965.

_____. *Topics in the theory of generative grammar*. The Hague: Mouton, 1966.

Cicirelli, V. G., Granger, R., Schemmel, D., Cooper, W., & Holthouse, N. Performance of disadvantaged primary-grade children on the revised Illinois Test of Psycholinguistic Abilities. *Psychology in the Schools*, 1971, **8**, 240–46.

Clasen, R. E., Spear, J. E., & Tomaro, M. P. A comparison of the relative effectiveness of two types of preschool compensatory programming. *The Journal of Educational Research*, 1969, **62**, 401–05.

Cruickshank, W., Bentzen, F., Ratzeberg, F., & Tannhauser, M. *A teaching method for brain-injured and hyperactive children*. Syracuse, N.Y.: Syracuse University Press, 1961.

Crutchfield, V. M. E. The effects of language training on the language development of mentally retarded children in Abilene State School. Unpublished doctoral dissertation, University of Denver, Denver, Colorado, 1964. *International Dissertation Abstracts*, 1964, **25**, 4572.

Deese, James. *Psycholinguistics*. Boston: Allyn & Bacon, 1971.

Deese, Jeanette. A study of the discrimination by the subtests of the revised Illinois Test of Psycholinguistic Abilities between successful and unsuccessful readers of normal intelligence. Unpublished doctoral dissertation, Memphis State University, Memphis, Tennessee, 1971.

Dickie, J. P. Effectiveness of structured and unstructured (traditional) methods of language training. In M. A. Brottman (Ed.), Language remediation for the disadvantaged pre-school child. *Monograph of the Society for Research in Child Development*, 1968, **33**, No. 124, 62–79.

Dillon, E. J. *An investigation of basic psycholinguistic and reading abilities among the cerebral palsied*. Unpublished doctoral dissertation, Temple University, Philadelphia, Pa. Ann Arbor, Mich.: University Microfilms, 1966, No. 66–9209.

Doughtie, E. B., Wakefield, J. A., Sampson, R. N., & Alston, H. L. A statistical test for the representational level of the Illinois Test of Psycholinguistic Ability. *Journal of Educational Psychology*, 1974, **66**, 410–15.

Dunn, L. M., & Mueller, M. W. The efficacy of the Initial Teaching Alphabet and the Peabody Language Development Kit with grade one disadvantaged children: After one year. IMRID papers and reports. Nashville, Tenn.: Institute on Mental Retardation and Intellectual Development, George Peabody College, 1966.

——————. Differential effects on the ITPA profile of the experimental version of level u1 of the Peabody Language Development Kits with disadvantaged first grade children. IMRID papers and reports. Nashville, Tenn.: Institute on Mental Retardation and Intellectual Development, George Peabody College, 1967.

Dunn, L. M., & Smith, J. O. *The Peabody Language Development Kits*. Circle Pines, Minn.: American Guidance Service, 1966.

Egeland, B., DiNello, M., & Carr, D. The relationship of intelligence, visual-motor, psycholinguistic, and reading readiness skills with achievement. *Educational and Psychological Measurement*, 1970, **30**, 451–58.

Elkins, J. Some psycholinguistic aspects of the differential diagnosis of reading disability in grades I and II. Unpublished doctoral dissertation, University of Queensland, Australia, 1972.

Ensminger, E. E. The effects of a classroom language development program on psycholinguistic abilities and intellectual functioning of slow learning and borderline retarded children. Unpublished doctoral dissertation, University of Kansas, Lawrence, 1966.

Estes, L. L. A comparative study of good and poor readers as shown by the Illinois Test of Psycholinguistic Abilities. Unpublished master's thesis, Chico State College, Chico, California, 1970.

Farrald, R. R., & Schamber, R. G. *Handbook 1: A mainstream approach to identification, assessment and amelioration of learning disabilities*. Sioux Falls, S. D.: Adapt, 1973.

Fernald, G. *Remedial techniques in basic school subjects*. New York: McGraw-Hill, 1943.

Ferrier, E. E. Investigation of the ITPA performance of children with functional deficits of articulation. *Exceptional Children*, 1966, **32**, 625–29.

Forgnone, C. Effects of visual perception and language training upon certain abilities of retarded children. Unpublished master's thesis, George Peabody College, Nashville, Tenn., 1966. *International Dissertation Abstracts*, 1967, **27**, 1197-A.

Foster, S. Language skills for children with persistent articulatory disorders. Unpublished doctoral dissertation, Texas Women's University, Denton, Texas, 1963.

Fries, C. C. *Linguistics and reading*. New York: Holt, Rinehart & Winston, 1963.

Frostig, M., & Horne, D. *The Frostig program for the development of visual perception: Teacher's guide*. Chicago: Follett, 1964.

Furth, H. G. Research with the deaf: Implications for language and cognition. *Psychological Bulletin*, 1964, **62**, 145–64.

Garrett, H. E. *Statistics in psychology and education*. New York: Longmans Green, 1954.

Gazdic, J. M. An evaluation of a program for those children ascertained to be not ready for regular first grade placement. Unpublished master's thesis, Northeastern Illinois State College, Chicago, Illinois, 1971.

Gibson, R. C. Effectiveness of a supplemental language development program with educable mentally retarded children. Unpublished doctoral dissertation, University of Iowa, Iowa City, 1966. *International Dissertation Abstracts*, 1967, **27**, 2726-A.

Giebink, J. W., & Marden, M. L. Verbal expression, verbal fluency, and grammar related to cultural experience. *Psychology in the Schools*, 1968, **5**, 365–68.

Gillingham, A., & Stillman, B. *Remedial training for children with specific disability in reading, spelling, and penmanship*. Cambridge, Mass.: Educators Publishing Service, 1965.

Glovsky, L. A comparison of two groups of mentally retarded children on the Illinois Test Psycholinguistic Abilities. *Training School Bulletin*, 1970, **67**, 4–14.

Golden, N. E., & Steiner, S. R. Auditory and visual functions in good and poor readers. *Journal of Learning Disabilities*, 1969, **2**, 476–81.

Goldstein, H., Moss, J. W., & Jordan, L. J. The efficacy of special class training on the development of mentally retarded children. Cooperative Research Project No. 619. Urbana, Ill.: University of Illinois, Institute for Research on Exceptional Children, 1965.

Goodstein, H. A., Whitney, G., & Cawley, J. F. Prediction of perceptual reading disability among disadvantaged children in the second grade. *The Reading Teacher*, 1970, **24**, 23–28.

Graubard, P. S. *Psycholinguistic correlates of reading disability in disturbed children*. Doctoral dissertation, Yeshiva University, New York, N. Y. Ann Arbor, Mich.: University Microfilms, 1965, No. 65–11,975.

Gray, S. W., & Klaus, R. A. An experimental preschool program for culturally deprived children. *Child Development*, 1965, 887–98.

Guess, D., Ensminger, E. E., & Smith, J. O. A language development program for mentally retarded children. Final report. Project No. 7–0815, Grant No. OEG–0–8–070815–0216 (032). Bureau of Education for the Handicapped, August 1969.

Guest, K. E. Relationships among the Illinois Test of Psycholinguistic Abilities, receptive and expressive language tasks, intelligence, and achievement. Unpublished doctoral dissertation, University of Wisconsin, Madison. Ann Arbor, Mich.: University Microfilms, 1971, No. 31(11-A), 5845.

Guilford, J. P. *Fundamental statistics in psychology and education*, New York: McGraw-Hill, 1956.

——————. Three faces of intellect. *The American Psychologist*, 1958, **8**, 469–79.

Guthrie, J. T., & Goldberg, H. K. Visual sequential-memory in reading disability. *Journal of Learning Disabilities*, 1972, **5**, 41–46.

Hallom, J. J. An exploratory study to determine the psycholinguistic abilities of a group of six-year-old children with severe articulation problems. Unpublished master's thesis, Sacramento State College, Sacramento, Calif., 1964.

Hammill, D. D., Larsen, S. C., Parker, R., Bagley, M. T., & Sanford, H. G. Perceptual and conceptual correlates of reading. Unpublished manuscript. University of Texas, Austin, 1974.

Hammill, D., Parker, R., & Newcomer, P. Psycholinguistic correlates of academic achievement. *Journal of School Psychology*, 1975, in press.

Hare, B., Hammill, D. D., & Bartel, N. Construct validity of selected ITPA subtests. *Exceptional Children*, 1973, **40**, 13–20.

Haring, N. G., & Ridgway, R. W. Early identification of children with learning disabilities. *Exceptional Children*, 1967, **33**, 387–95.

Hart, N. W. M. The differential diagnosis of the psycholinguistic abilities of the cerebral palsied child and effective remedial procedures. *Special Schools Bulletin*, No. 2, Brisbane, Australia, 1963.

Hartman, A. S. A long-range attack to reduce the educational disadvantage of children from poverty backgrounds, 1965–66, Progress Report to the Ford Foundation. Harrisburg, Pa.: Department of Public Instruction, 1967.

Hatch, E., & French, J. L. Revised ITPA: Its reliability and validity for use with EMRs. *Journal of School Psychology*. 1971, **9**, 16–23.

Hepburn, A. W. The performance of normal children of differing reading ability on the Illinois Test of Psycholinguistic Abilities. Unpublished doctoral dissertation, University of Minnesota, Minneapolis. Ann Arbor, Mich.: University Microfilms, 1968, No. 68–71,685.

Hirshoren, A. A comparison of the predictive validity of the Revised Stanford-Binet Intelligence Scale and the Illinois Test of Psycholinguistic Abilities. *Exceptional Children*, 1969, **25**, 517–21.

Hodges, W. L., & Spicker, H. H. The effects of preschool experiences on culturally disadvantaged children. In W. W. Hartub, and N. L. Smothergill (Eds.), *The young child: Review of research*. Washington, D.C.: National Association for the Education of Young Children, 1967. Pp. 262–89.

Horner, R. D. A factor analysis comparison of the ITPA and PLS with mentally retarded children. *Exceptional Children*, 1967, **34**, 183–89.

Hubschman, E., Polizzotto, E. A., & Kaliski, M. S. Performance of institutionalized retardates on the PPVT and two editions of the ITPA. *American Journal of Mental Deficiency*, 1970, **74**, 579–80.

Hunt, J. McV. *Intelligence and experience*. New York: Ronald, 1961.

Hyatt, G. L. S. Some psycholinguistic characteristics of first graders who have reading problems at the end of second grade. Unpublished doctoral dissertation, University of Oregon, Eugene. Ann Arbor, Mich.: University Microfilms, 1968, No. 69–26.

Hyman, R. T. *Ways of teaching*. Philadelphia: Lippincott, 1974.

Ikeda, M. The relationship between the Illinois Test of Psycholinguistic Abilities, reading performance, and IQ of third-grade children. Doctoral dissertation, University of New Mexico, Las Cruces. Ann Arbor, Mich.: University Microfilms, 1970, No. 71–9279.

Jastak, J. F., & Jastak, S. R. *The Wide Range Achievement Test: Manual of instruction*. Wilmington, Del.: Guidance Associates, 1965.

Johnson, D., & Myklebust, H. *Learning disabilities: Educational principles and practices*. New York: Grune & Stratton, 1967.

Jones, E. L. H. The effects of a language development program on the psycholinguistic abilities and IQ of a group of preschool disadvantaged children. Unpublished doctoral dissertation, University of Arkansas, Fayetteville, 1970. *International Dissertation Abstracts*, 1970, **31**, 2761-A.

Jorstad, D. Psycholinguistic learning disabilities in 20 Mexican-American students. *Journal of Learning Disabilities*, 1971, **4**, 143–49.

Karnes, M. B. *Activities for developing psycholinguistic skills with preschool culturally disadvantaged children*. Washington, D.C.: Council for Exceptional Children, 1968.

——————. *Goal Program: Language development*. Springfield, Mass.: Milton Bradley, 1972.

Karnes, M. B., Teska, J. A., & Hodgins, A. S. The effects of four programs of classroom intervention on intellectual and language development of four-year-old disadvantaged children. *American Journal of Orthopsychiatry*, 1970, **40**, 58–76.

Kass, C. E. Psycholinguistic disabilities of children with reading problems. *Exceptional Children*, 1966, **32**, 533–39.

Katz, J. J., & Fodor, J. A. The structure of a semantic theory. *Language*, 1963, **39**, 170–210.

Kier, S. M. A comparison of the psycholinguistic abilities of mentally retarded word-recognizers and mentally retarded slow readers. Unpublished doctoral dissertation, Sacramento State College, Sacramento, Calif., 1963.

Kiniry, S. Differentiating elementary children with learning disabilities using the Illinois Test of Psycholinguistic Abilities. Unpublished doctoral dissertation, East Texas State University, Commerce, Texas, 1972.

Kirk, S. A. *Educating exceptional children*. New York: Houghton-Mifflin, 1972.

Kirk, S. A., & Bateman, B. *Ten years of research at the Institute for Research on Exceptional Children*. Urbana, Ill.: University of Illinois Press, 1964.

Kirk, S. A., & Kirk, W. D. *Psycholinguistic learning disabilities: Diagnosis and remediation*. Urbana, Ill.: University of Illinois Press, 1971.

Kirk, S. A., & McCarthy, J. J. The Illinois Test of Psycholinguistic Abilities: An approach to differential diagnosis. In R. L. Jones (Ed.), *New directions in special education*. Boston: Allyn & Bacon, 1970. Pp. 102–22.

Kirk, S. A., McCarthy, J. J., & Kirk, W. D. *Illinois Test of Psycholinguistic Abilities*. Urbana, Ill.: University of Illinois Press, 1968.

Kirk, S. A., & McLeod, J. Research studies in psycholinguistic research. Selected conference papers. Washington, D.C.: Council for Exceptional Children, 1966.

Kuske, I. I., Jr. Psycholinguistic abilities of Sioux Indian children. Unpublished doctoral dissertation, University of South Dakota, Vermillion. Ann Arbor, Mich.: University Microfilms, 1969, No. 70–5304.

Larsen, S. C., Rogers, D., & Sowell, V. An investigation of various perceptual tests differentiating between normal and learning disabled children. Unpublished manuscript, The University of Texas, Austin, 1974.

Lashley, K. S. The problem of serial order in behavior. In L. A. Jeffress (Ed.), *Cerebral mechanisms in behavior*. New York: Wiley, 1951. Pp. 112–36.

Lavin, C. M. The effects of a structured sensory-motor training program on selected cognitive and psycholinguistic abilities of preschool children. Unpublished doctoral dissertation, Fordham University, Bronx, New York. *International Dissertation Abstracts*, 1971, **32**, 1984-A.

Lee, L. *Northwest Syntax Screening Test*. Evanston, Ill.: Northwestern University Press, 1969.

Leiss, R. H. The effect of intensity in a psycholinguistic stimulation program for trainable mentally retarded children. Unpublished doctoral dissertation, Temple University, Philadelphia, Pa., 1974.

Leong, C. K. If the model fits: An analysis of the structure of the revised Illinois Test of Psycholinguistic Abilities for moderately mentally retarded children. *Slow Learning Child*, 1974, **21**, 100–13.

Leton, D. A. A factor analysis of the ITPA and WISC scores of learning disabled pupils. *Psychology in the Schools*, 1972, **8**, 31–36.

Leventhal, D. S., & Stedman, D. J. A factor analytic study of the Illinois Test of Psycholinguistic Abilities. *Journal of Clinical Psychology*, 1970, **26**, 473–77.

Lombardi, T. P. Psycholinguistic abilities of Papago Indian school children. *Exceptional Children*, 1970, **36**, 485–93.

Luria, A. R. Neuropsychological analysis of focal brain lesions. In B. B. Wolman (Ed.), *Handbook of clinical psychology*. New York: McGraw-Hill, 1965.

Macione, J. R. Psychological correlates of reading disability as defined by the Illinois Test of Psycholinguistic Abilities. Unpublished doctoral dissertation, University of South Dakota, Vermillion. Ann Arbor, Mich.: University Microfilms, 1969, No. 70–5308.

Mann, L. Psychometric phrenology and the new faculty psychology: The case against ability assessment and training. *The Journal of Special Education*, 1971, **5**, 3–14.

Mann, L., & Phillips, W. A. Fractional practices in special education: A critique. *Exceptional Children*, 1967, **33**, 311–19.

McCarron, L. T. Psycholinguistic profiles of Mexican-American disadvantaged children. Paper presented at the annual meeting of the Western Psychological Association, San Francisco, April 1971.

McCarthy, J. J. Patterns of psycholinguistic development of mongoloid and nonmongoloid severely retarded children. Unpublished doctoral dissertation, University of Illinois, Urbana. Ann Arbor, Mich.: University Microfilms, 1965, No. 65–7134.

McCarthy, J. J., & Kirk, S. A. *The Illinois Test of Psycholinguistic Abilities. Examiners' manual*. Urbana: Ill.: University of Illinois Press, 1961.

McCarthy, J. J., & Olson, J. L. *Validity studies on the Illinois Test of Psycholinguistic Abilities*. Urbana, Ill.: University of Illinois Press, 1963.

McConnell, F., Horton, K. B., & Smith, B. R. Effects of early language training for culturally disadvantaged preschool children. *The Journal of School Health*, 1969, **39**, 661–65; *See also*: Language development and culturally disadvantaged. *Exceptional Children*, 1969, **35**, 597–606; *See also*: Sensory-perceptual and language training to prevent school learning disabilities in culturally deprived preschool children. Final report, Project No.: 5–0682. Grant No. OEG–32–52–7900–5025, USOE Bureau of Research. The Bill Wilkerson Hearing and Speech Center, Nashville, Tenn., August 1972.

McKeachie, W. J., & Doyle, C. L. *Psychology*. Reading, Mass.: Addison-Wesley, 1966.

McLean, J. E., Yoder, D. E., & Schiefelbush, R. L. (Eds.) *Language intervention with the retarded: Developing strategies.* Baltimore, Md.: University Park Press, 1972.

McLeod, J. Some psychological and psycholinguistic aspects of severe reading disability in children. Unpublished doctoral dissertation, University of Queensland, Australia, 1965.

_____. Psychological and psycholinguistic aspects of severe reading disability in children: Some experimental approaches. In *International approach to learning disabilities in children and youth*. Proceedings of the American Association for Children with Learning Disabilities annual convention, Tulsa, Oklahoma, 1966a.

_____. Dyslexia in young children. A factorial study with special reference to the Illinois Test of Psycholinguistic Abilities. *IREC Papers in Education,* Vol. 2, No. 1. Urbana, Ill.: University of Illinois Press, 1966b.

_____. (Ed.) *The slow learner in the primary school.* Sydney: Novak, 1968.

_____. Review of the month. *Rehabilitation Literature,* 1970, **31**, 16–18.

Mecham, M. J., Jex, J. L., & Jones, J. D. *Utah Test of Language Development.* Salt Lake City, Utah: Communication Research Associates, 1967.

Merlin, S. B. The psycholinguistic and reading abilities of educable mentally retarded readers. Unpublished doctoral dissertation, West Virginia University, Morgantown. Ann Arbor, Mich.: University Microfilms, 1971, No. 71–26,632.

Meyers, C. E. What the ITPA measures: A synthesis of factor studies of the 1961 edition. *Educational Psychological Measurement,* 1969, **29**, 867–76.

Milgram, N. A. A note on the PPVT in mental retardates. *American Journal of Mental Deficiency,* 1967, **72**, 496–97.

Minskoff, E. H. Creating and evaluating remediation for the learning disabled. *Focus on Exceptional Children,* 1973, **5**.

_____. Remediating auditory-verbal learning disabilities: The role of teacher-pupil verbal interaction. *Journal of Learning Disabilities,* 1974, **7**, 406–13.

Minskoff, E. H., & Minskoff, J. G. Remedial and compensatory teaching: A critical view of the roles and responsibilities of special and general education. Unpublished paper. Hopkins, Minn.: 2½ Webster Place, 1974.

Minskoff, E. H., Wiseman, D. E., & Minskoff, J. G. *The MWM program for developing language abilities.* Ridgefield, N. J.: Educational Performance Associates, 1972.

Minskoff, J. G. The effectiveness of a specific program based on language diagnosis in overcoming learning disabilities of mentally retarded— emotionally disturbed children. USOE Project No. 6–8375, Grant No. OEG–1–6–068375–1550, May 1967. *See also*: A psycholinguistic approach to remediation with retarded-disturbed children. Unpublished doctoral dissertation, Yeshiva University, New York, N. Y., 1967. *International Dissertation Abstracts*, 1967, **28**, 1625-A.

Mitchell, R. S. A study of the effects of specific training in psycholinguistic scores of Head Start children. Unpublished doctoral dissertation. *International Dissertation Abstracts*, 1968, **28**, 1709-A.

Mittler, P., & Ward, J. The use of the Illinois Test of Psycholinguistic Abilities on British four-year-old children: A normative and factorial study. *British Journal of Educational Psychology*, 1970, **40**, 43–54.

Money, J. Editorial. *Journal of Learning Disabilities*, 1969, **2**, 144–45.

Monterey Language Program. Monterey, Calif.: Behavorial Science Institute, 1972.

Morgan, D. L. A comparison of growth in language development in a structured and traditional preschool compensatory education program. Unpublished doctoral dissertation, United States International University, San Diego, Calif., 1971. *International Dissertation Abstracts*, 1971, **31**, 4388-A.

Morris, S. K. Results of a study using the Peabody Language Development Kit: Level P. Experimental Edition. Unpublished master's thesis, Vanderbilt University, Nashville, Tenn., 1967.

Mueller, M. W. Language profiles of mentally retarded children. Selected convention papers, Forty-second Annual Council for Exceptional Children Convention, Chicago, March 1964.

_____. A comparison of the empirical validity of six tests of ability with educable mental retardates. Nashville, Tenn.: George Peabody College for Teachers, 1965.

_____. Prediction of achievement of educable mentally retarded children. *American Journal of Mental Deficiency*, 1969, **73**, 590–96.

Mueller, M. W., & Dunn, L. W. Effects of level #1 of the Peabody Language Development Kits with educable mentally retarded children—an interim report after 4½ months. IMRID papers and reports. Nashville, Tenn.: Institute on Mental Retardation and Intellectual Development, George Peabody College, 1967.

Mueller, M. W., & Weaver, S. J. Psycholinguistic abilities of institutionalized and non-institutionalized trainable mental retardates. *American Journal of Mental Deficiency*, 1964, **68**, 775–83.

Myers, P. I. A study of language disabilities in cerebral palsied children. *Journal of Speech and Hearing Research*, 1965, **8**, 129–37.

Myklebust, H. R. *Progress in learning disabilities, Vol. 1.* New York: Grune & Stratton, 1967.

———. *Auditory disorders in children: A manual for differential diagnosis.* New York: Grune & Stratton, 1954.

Newcomer, P. L. Construct validity of the Illinois Test of Psycholinguistic Abilities. Unpublished doctoral dissertation, Temple University, Philadelphia, Pa., 1973.

Newcomer, P., & Hammill, D. A short form of the Illinois Test of Psycholinguistic Abilities. *Journal of Learning Disabilities,* 1974, **7**, 570–72.

Newcomer, P., Hare, B., Hammill, D., & McGettigan, J. Construct validity of the Illinois Test of Psycholinguistic Abilities. *Journal of Learning Disabilities,* 1975, **8**, 220–31.

Olson, J. L. Deaf and sensory aphasic children. *Exceptional Children,* 1961, **27**, 422–24.

Osgood, C. E. Motivational dynamics of language behavior. In M. R. Jones (Ed.), *Nebraska symposium on motivation.* Lincoln, Neb.: University of Nebraska Press, 1957.

———. A behavioristic analysis of perception and language as cognitive phenomena. In *Contemporary approaches to cognition: The Colorado symposium.* Cambridge, Mass.: Harvard University Press, 1957b.

———. "Where do sentences come from?" In D. D. Steinberg, & L. A. Jakobovits (Eds.), *Semantics: An interdisciplinary reader in philosophy, linguistics and psychology. Cambridge:* Cambridge University Press, 1971.

Osgood, C. E., & Miron, M. S. (Eds.) *Approaches to the study of aphasia.* Urbana, Ill.: University of Illinois Press, 1963.

Osgood, C. E., & Sebeok (Eds.) Psycholinguistics. Supplement, *Journal of Abnormal and Social Psychology,* 1954, **52**.

Painter, G. The effect of a rhythmic and sensory motor activity program on perceptual motor spatial abilities of kindergarten children. *Exceptional Children,* 1966, **33**, 113–16.

Paraskevopoulos, J. N., & Kirk, S. A. *The development and psychometric characteristics of the revised Illinois Test of Psycholinguistic Abilities.* Urbana, Ill.: University of Illinois Press, 1969.

Parker, R. A program of Scheffé's method. *Educational and Psychological Measurement,* 1971, **31**, 761.

Pasamanick, B., & Knobloch, H. Epidemilogic studies on the complication of pregnancies and the birth process. In G. Kaplan (Ed.), *Prevention of mental disorders in children.* New York: Basic, 1961.

Piaget, J. *The language and thought of the child.* New York: Meridian, 1955.

Proger, B. B., Cross, L. H., & Burger, R. M. Construct validation of standardized tests in special education: A framework of reference and application to ITPA research (1967–1971). In L. Mann, & D. Sabatino (Eds.), *The first review of Special Education*. Philadelphia: JSE Press, 1973. Pp. 165–202.

Pumfrey, P. D., & Naylor, J. G. The psycholinguistic disabilities of poor readers: Their diagnosis and remediation. Unpublished manuscript, Department of Education, University of Manchester, England, 1975.

Ragland, G. The performance of educable mentally handicapped students of different reading ability on the ITPA. *Selected convention papers*. Forty-fourth Annual Convention of the Council for Exceptional Children. Washington, D.C., 1966.

Reichstein, J. Auditory threshold consistency: A basic characteristic for differential diagnoses of children with communication disorders. Unpublished doctoral dissertation, Teacher College, Columbia University, New York, N.Y., 1963.

Rosenberg, S. Problems of language development in the retarded. In H. C. Haywood (Ed.), *Social-cultural aspects of mental retardation*. New York: Appleton-Century-Crofts, 1970. Pp. 203–216.

Rosenfield, A. G. Psycholinguistic abilities as predictors of reading ability and disability: How valid is the ITPA? Paper presented at the American Educational Research Association Annual Convention, New York, February 1971.

Ruhly, V. M. A study of the relationship of self-concept, socioeconomic background and psycholinguistic abilities to reading achievement of second grade males residing in a suburban area. Unpublished doctoral dissertation, Wayne State University, Detroit, Mich. Ann Arbor, Mich.: University Microfilms, 1970, No. 71–448.

Runyon, M. J. L. The effects of a psycholinguistic development language program on language abilities of educable mentally retarded children. Unpublished master's thesis, Cardinal Stritch College, Milwaukee, Wis., 1970.

Ryckman, D. B. Psychological processes of disadvantaged children. Unpublished doctoral dissertation, University of Illinois, Urbana, 1966.

Ryckman, D. B., & Wiegerink, R. The factors of the Illinois Test of Psycholinguistic Abilities: A comparison of 18 factor analyses. *Exceptional Children*, 1969, **36**, 107–13.

Sabatino, D., & Hayden, D. Variation in information processing behaviors. *Journal of Learning Disabilities*, 1970, **3**, 404–12.

Saudargas, R. A., Madsen, C. H., & Thompson, F. Prescriptive teaching in language arts remediation for black rural elementary school children. *Journal of Learning Disabilities*, 1970, **3**, 364–70.

Sapir, S. G. Learning disability and deficit centered classroom training. In J. Hellmuth (Ed.), *Deficits in cognition*. New York: Brunner-Mazel, 1971. Pp. 324–37.

Schiefelbusch, R. L. (Ed.) *Language of the mentally retarded*. Baltimore, Md.: University Park Press, 1972.

Schifani, J. W. The relationship between the Illinois Test of Psycholinguistic Abilities and the Peabody Language Development Kit with a select group of intermediate educable mentally retarded children. Unpublished doctoral dissertation, University of Alabama, Tuscaloosa, 1971. *International Dissertation Abstracts*, 1972, **32**, 5076-A.

Sears, C. R. A comparison of the basic language concepts and psycholinguistic abilities of second grade boys who demonstrate average and below average levels of reading achievement. Unpublished doctoral dissertation, Colorado State College, Ft. Collins. Ann Arbor, Mich.: University Microfilms, 1969, No. 16–19, 233.

Sedlak, R. A., & Weener, P. Review of research on the Illinois Test of Psycholinguistic Abilities. In Mann, L., & Sabatino, D. A. (Eds.), *The first review of special education*. Philadelphia, Pa., JSE Press, 1973. Pp. 113–64.

Semmel, M. I., & Mueller, M. W. A factor analysis of the ITPA with mentally retarded children. In B. Bateman (Ed.), *The ITPA in current research: Summary of studies*. Urbana, Ill.: University of Illinois Press, 1965.

Serwer, B. L., & Badian, N. A. The Illinois Test of Psycholinguistic Abilities as a predictive instrument for a sample of learning disability children. Unpublished manuscript, Boston University, Boston, Mass., no date.

Siders, S. K. An analysis of the language growth of selected children in a first grade Title 1 project. Unpublished doctoral dissertation, Kent State University, Kent, Ohio, 1969. *International Dissertation Abstracts*, 1970, **30**, 4158-A.

Skinner, B. F. *Verbal behavior*. New York: Appleton-Century-Crofts, 1957.

Smith, J. M. Utilization of the Illinois Test of Psycholinguistic Abilities with educationally handicapped children. Unpublished doctoral dissertation, University of the Pacific, Stockton, Calif. Ann Arbor, Mich.: University Microfilms, 1970, No. 70–23, 254.

Smith, J. O. Group language development for educable mental retardates. *Exceptional Children*, 1962, **29**, 95–101.

Smith, P. A., & Marx, R. W. Factor structure of the revised edition of the Illinois Test of Psycholinguistic Abilities. *Psychology in the Schools*, 1971, **8**, 349–56.

Smith, R. M., & McWilliams, B. J. Psycholinguistic abilities of children with clefts. *Cleft Palate Journal*, 1968 **5**, 238–49.

Sowell, V. The efficacy of psycholinguistic training through the MWM program. Unpublished doctoral dissertation, University of Texas, Austin, 1975.

Sowell, V., & Larsen, S. Relationship of perceptual skills to reading. Unpublished manuscript, University of Texas, Austin, 1974.

Spollen, J. C., & Ballif, B. L. Effectiveness of individualized instruction for kindergarten children with a developmental lag. *Exceptional Children*, 1971, **38**, 205–9.

Spradlin, J. E. Assessment of speech and language of retarded children: The Parson Language Scales. *Journal of Speech and Hearing Disorders*, 1963. Monograph Supplement #10, 8–31.

Stearns, K. E. Experimental group language development for psycho-socially deprived preschool children. Unpublished doctoral dissertation, Indiana University, Bloomington, 1966. *International Dissertation Abstracts*, 1967, **27**, 2078-A.

Stephenson, B. L., & Gay, W. D. Psycholinguistic abilities of black and white children from four SES levels. *Exceptional Children*, 1972, **38**, 705–9.

Strauss, A. A., & Lehtinen, L. E. *Psychopathology and education of the brain-injured child, Vol. 1.* New York: Grune & Stratton, 1947.

Strauss, A. A., & Kephart, N. C. *Psychopathology and education of the brain-injured child. Vol. 2.* New York: Grune & Stratton, 1955.

Strickland, J. H. The effect of a parent education program on the language development of underprivileged kindergarten children. Unpublished doctoral dissertation, George Peabody College, Nashville, Tenn., 1967. *International Dissertation Abstracts*, 1967, **28**, 1633-A.

Sumner, J. W. A comparison of some psycholinguistic abilities of educable mentally retarded readers and non-readers. Unpublished doctoral dissertation, University of North Carolina, Chapel Hill. Ann Arbor, Mich.: University Microfilms, 1966, No. 67–1055.

Teasdale, G. R., & Katz, F. M. Psycholinguistic abilities of children from different ethnic and socioeconomic backgrounds. *Australian Journal of Psychology*, 1968, **20**, 155–59.

Thurstone, L. L. Psychological implications of factor analysis. *American Psychologist*, 1948, **3**, 402–8.

Vygotsky, L. S. *Thought and language.* Cambridge, Mass.: MIT Press, 1962.

Warden, P. G. The validity of the Illinois Test Psycholinguistic Abilities as a predictor of academic achievement of first grade students. Unpublished master's thesis, Kent State University, Kent, Ohio, 1967.

Washington, E. D., & Teska, J. A. Correlations between the Wide Range Achievement Test, the California Achievement Tests, the Stanford-Binet, and the Illinois Test of Psycholinguistic Abilities. *Psychological Reports*, 1970, **26**, 291–94.

Waugh, R. Comparison of revised and experimental editions of the ITPA. *Journal of Learning Disabilities*, 1973, **6**, 236–38.

Weaver, S. J., & Weaver, A. Psycholinguistic abilities of culturally deprived Negro children. *American Journal of Mental Deficiency*, 1967, **72**, 190–97.

Webb, P. K. A comparison of the psycholinguistic abilities of Anglo-American, Negro, and Latin-American lower-class preschool children. Unpublished doctoral dissertation, North Texas State University, Denton, Texas. Ann Arbor, Mich.: University Microfilms, 1968, No. 29(10-A), 3351–52.

Wepman, J. M., Jones, L. V., Bock, R. D., & Van Pelt, D. Studies in aphasia: Background and theoretical formulations. In L. A. Jakobovits and M. S. Miron (Eds.), *Readings in the psychology of language*. Englewood Cliffs, N. J.: Prentice-Hall, 1964.

Westinghouse Learning Corporation/Ohio University. *The impact of Head Start on children's cognitive and affective development*, Vols. 1 & 2. Springfield, Va.: U.S. Department of Commerce Clearinghouse, 1969.

Wiseman, D. E. The effects of an individualized remedial program on mentally retarded children with psycholinguistic disabilities. Unpublished doctoral dissertation, University of Illinois, Urbana, 1965. *International Dissertation Abstracts*, 1965, **26**, 5143-A.

Wisland, M., & Many, W. A. A factorial study of the Illinois Test of Psycholinguistic Abilities with children having above average intelligence. *Educational and Psychological Measurement*, 1969, **29**, 367–76.

Wright, L. S. Perceptual and cognitive characteristics and their relationship to social factors and academic achievement in third grade conduct problem boys. Unpublished doctoral dissertation, University of Illinois, Urbana. Ann Arbor, Mich.: University Microfilms, 1970, No. 31(2-A), 572.

Zangwill, O. L. *Cerebral dominance and its relation to psychological function*. Edinburgh: Oliver & Bond, 1960.

Zbinden, W. R. Psycholinguistic and perceptual correlates of spelling in educable mentally handicapped children. Unpublished doctoral dissertation, University of Illinois, Urbana. Ann Arbor, Mich.: University Microfilms, 1970, No. 70–21,092.

Author Index

179

DATE DUE			